PICTURE FRAMING

A Practical Guide from Basic to Baroque

PICTURE FRAMING

A Practical Guide from Basic to Baroque

Desmond MacNamara

David & Charles
Newton Abbot London North Pomfret (Vt)

© DESMOND MAC NAMARA 1986
BRITISH LIBRARY CATALOGUING IN
PUBLICATION DATA

Mac Namara, Desmond
  Picture Framing: a practical guide from
  basic to Baroque
  1. Picture Frames and Framing – Amateurs
  manuals
  749.7   N8550

  ISBN 0-7153-8689-1

Designed by Laurence Bradbury

Printed in the Netherlands by Royal Smeets
Offset BV, Weert

CONTENTS

INTRODUCTION

THERE HAVE BEEN many books on practical picture framing, published in Britain and America. The best of them emphasize the importance of proportion, choice of mouldings, textures, colour and finishes, and make some effort to point the reader in an imaginative direction. Others, alas, offer little more than advice on chopping up bits of ready-made moulding and assembling them into rectangles, or cutting holes in sheets of board – the least part of the whole business. A well-framed picture on which thought and skill have been lavished should have double the sensual impact of a picture neatly boxed by a competent local framer. The difference is not a matter of cost, as I hope to show. Quite the reverse. The added factor is made up of judgment, knowledge, invention and the few dozen tricks that underlie the practice of any art. I can only point to the former and attempt to explain something of the latter.

When, by chance as much as anything, I first undertook to teach picture framing to adults, I quickly realized that there was little to teach except some specialized carpentry and the rudiments of taste and proportion. When I tried to extend this I came up against the high cost of mouldings, inconvenient expeditions to specialized shops and difficult choices. Many of the mouldings that satisfied my criterion were beyond the pockets of my students and were in any case pitifully few in number. When someone brought a tolerable copy of a Goya pastoral, no one could supply the elements of a Spanish baroque frame which would have made the picture a striking mural event.

I began to break this tyranny of supply by guiding some students to frame a few National Gallery Italian renaissance prints in an appropriate manner, using simple pieces of timber from a DIY shop and some gesso, colour and so forth. The main tool, apart from saw, hammer etc., was a sharp stylus made from a 2-inch (50-mm) nail for engraving the chaste design in gesso on the centre flat area (a piece of two-by-one/50 × 25-mm timber) with the help of a stencil cut in a strip of copper. When it worked, the excitement it engendered in the class drove me to exploring available public collections of paintings to see if I could extend my capacities.

I cannot pretend that I enjoy all the framing in the great national collections, but I saw many mouldings which could not be bought but which my students would be eager to use if this were remotely possible. I also realized that some speeding up of traditional methods was needed for students who only spent a few hours a week in my company. Many traditional materials and methods could not be bettered and had to be used, but some could be advantageously adapted, although not improved, by using modern sculptural techniques. This principle came to me one day when I began to think of a frame moulding as a narrow sculptural or architectural frieze.

From the 15th century to the third quarter of the 18th century nearly all frames were carved in wood, but there were exceptions. Added ornament in a sort of stucco composition was described in detail by Cellino Cellini in the 15th century, cast from terra cotta reverse moulds. In the 16th century in Italy, and probably in France, reproduced designs of this kind were used in small framing and in the elaborate theatrical occasions, masques and the like, which were part of royal or ducal weddings – acres of painted backdrops, triumphal arches, temples, statues, gods, chariots and costumes, enlivened by ballets of naked nymphs and tritons.

In the second half of the 18th century in France, carved wooden frames were chiselled very roughly in soft wood and coated heavily with gesso which was itself carved and sharpened by specialists. At about the same time the practice of adding ornament in *papier maché* and gesso composition began to spread, with the effulgence of rococo ornament. This produced an anti-French backlash in England on the part of English designers like Johnson and Chippendale, both of whom were notable frame designers as well as furniture makers. But the process of adding ornament was too economic to be a passing fashion, and the increasing demand for framing on the part of the middle class in Europe throughout the 19th century meant that the practice had come to stay.

When seeking to enlarge the repertoire of moulding designs for my students, I was downcast at the number of elegant and useful patterns made by good craftsmen long since dead, and sought to find some way of revitalizing their ghosts. This had to be done in such a way that it could be carried out within the confines of a class, without subdivisions of labour or inordinately lengthy apprenticeships. In the pursuit of this aim, I discovered that some repeating patterns on mouldings could be copied, in clay or wax, given some modelling skill. One unit of design might be no more than a few inches long, and several casts of this, joined length to length and patched at the joints, produced a length of moulding about 3 feet (1 m) long, a convenient length for storing. By the same token an agreeable and suitable design could be abstracted from a Chinese urn, a Persian tile or a New Guinea bark cloth and reassembled as a running pattern for a picture frame moulding that a Sung Chinese or a Persian miniaturist would not have envizaged, but would instantly recognize.

In the pages that follow I attempt to describe the result of these endeavours, starting from four pieces of timber and utilizing some extremely decorative period mouldings with a variety of finishes, largely of my own devising. The repair or reconstruction of damaged frames is also described, using a combination of new materials with those that have proved their superiority for more than five hundred years.

I make no bones about the fact that I am describing a hundred or so conjuring tricks, mostly but not all of my own devising, and can only point the way towards experience and aesthetic judgment. For a beginning I can only recommend visits to national collections. Some knowledge of the history of Western art is invaluable, indeed essential, but this is acquired gradually. Hopefully the quest will prove exciting. Everything described has been fully tested with adult students of very mixed ability, and they all work, sometimes spectacularly well. This book has to confine itself to the subject, perforce

Leonardo Da Vinci (1452–1519). La Gioconda. This is the last of several frames lost during thefts, but it is correct for the turn of the 16th century: the later Renaissance

narrowly, so I cannot include a chapter on devising a new moulding design. I know, however, that some readers will have some skill in this direction and I have attempted to show them how to use and adapt it. A picture frame or a mirror glass frame is really linear sculpture, deriving from architectural design and echoing the furniture of a given period.

Sadly, too many people, including some who should know better, have a very sketchy understanding of the development of framing down the centuries. Some knowledge of its historical development needs to be balanced against other criteria, such as aesthetic judgment, ambience and mother wit, in deciding how to frame a painting, a drawing or any flat image. Fashion, like the law, is 'an ass', as Charles Dickens described it; nonetheless it merits considerable respect. Simplicity in itself is not a merit, as a generation of architects has discovered, nor is overloaded design. Prejudice in both of these directions is common and obscures good judgment.

The practice of picture framing is now world-wide but this is a fairly recent development. It developed in Europe over the last five hundred years from architectural design, of which it is a part. Elsewhere in the world, sophisticated schools of painting developed which did not involve framing or hanging pictures on walls. Apart from fresco painting on lime plaster walls, Persian, Chinese, Japanese, Indian or Mogul paintings were not hung. Some were kept in folios, some stored in chests, to be taken out and enjoyed on suitable occasions. Nowadays, social habits having changed, all such precious objects would be safely framed and displayed or, I fear, locked away in a bank vault.

Early examples of framing
Since no classical panel painting remains, apart from the encaustic Roman mummy portraits found at Fayum, Egypt, there is no evidence of framing. However, many of the fresco panels painted on the walls of Pompeii and nearby cities are surrounded by light and dark lines resembling some 17th-century gallery frames. There are examples of small fresco panels framed in stucco cornices remarkably resembling frames carved in wood.

Examples of these are numerous. There is a wall panel of Orpheus charming the beasts in mosaic in the Palermo Museum. It is surrounded by a mosaic 'frame' of a twisted rope pattern set on a flat between an inner and outer ridge. Executed in wood, such a frame was common from the 17th century onwards. In the Naples Museum there is a landscape panel from Herculaneum 'framed' in a painted red border of three red lines, like many 17th-century gallery frames. A small relief of the building of the ship Argo from the Villa Albani is framed in an oval beading in stucco that would not have seemed out of place in the court of Louis XVI.

But there are endless such examples. When we consider that many architectural features in classical times were stone developments from wooden originals, and that painting was a cheap form of sculpture, it seems reasonable to assume that when we look at these 'frames' in mosaic, stucco or fresco, we are looking at representations of wooden frames.

The panel painting did not play a large part in classical art, nor did it in the centuries that followed the fragmentation and collapse of the Roman Empire, but the idea of a decorative border around a manuscript painting was common.

The Irish monks of Iona adapted Christian symbols to the whorls and convolutions that their ancestors had used for centuries, and the decorative border was a common feature of their extraordinary art. The St. John page of the 9th-century Book of Kells shows the saint, highly conventionalized, but surrounded by a border which, remarkably, resembles the rhythms and proportions of a 17th-century baroque frame; a Louis XIV corner and centre ornaments are identical. This is coincidence, but whether on vellum or on plastered walls, the idea that a painted image of a scene that emanates from an artist's mind needs a boundary line or border to enclose it seems deeply ingrained in European culture. The world of the painter's imagination cannot be allowed to sprawl onto the hewn stone blocks of reality and must be contained within a border.

A SHORT HISTORY OF PICTURE FRAMING

THIS BRIEF SUMMARY of the history of European framing is intended as a guide, a synopsis of the subject, useful to students visiting national collections in any country, from Edinburgh to Rome. Its purpose is to suggest the evolution in painting and taste and to draw attention to the fact that there is a vast reservoir of design to be understood, adapted or taken into account. The more you know the better your judgment.

Early panel paintings in the 13th and 14th centuries were votive and often in triptych form: a painting with a centre panel and two hinged side panels with a major and two subsidiary subjects as in the Duccio Madonna from the National Gallery, London. These were small enough to be portable and often used for portable altars.

In the 15th-century panel painting had become more fashionable and advanced in technique. It is at this time that framing developed in two different directions, and the results of this are still in evidence today. In Flemish merchant towns like Bruges or Ghent a realistic school of painting with a linear style developed, featuring religious subjects for altar use and secular portraits. The secularization of treatment, even for religious purposes, was essential to advance the art of painting past the static imagery of the icon or the mosaic.

These northern painters set their work in very simple wooden mouldings, ideally suited to the panelled merchants' homes, churches and almshouses in which they hung. The portrait by Robert Campin (1387–1455) and the 'Man in a Turban' by Jan van Eyck (1390–1441) from the National Gallery, London both exemplify this, but the suitability of this light Flemish framing is instantly apparent if one visits the Memling Museum or the Hôpital St. Jean by the intersecting canals of Bruges in Belgium, a city like the coloured toyland of a Gothic illuminated manuscript.

In Italy, the Dominican monk Fra Angelico (1387–1445) was a contemporary of Campin. His style, though tender, was very conservative by Florentine standards. Nevertheless, the difference in mood and scale between Flanders and Tuscany can be seen by anyone immediately. A generation later the whole drift of Renaissance taste is more apparent. Still Gothic in feeling and paid for by trade, the framing of the 'Madonna della Rondine' by Carlo Crivelli, the Venetian painter (c. 1430–95) reflects a different world; not better or worse but imbued with classical pretensions which perhaps never died in Italy. This kind of early Renaissance frame is called an 'aedicula' from the Latin 'aedes', a public building; a Roman dolls' house for a Virgin and a swallow.

Within a few decades the pilasters had shrunk to low relief, the cornice had disappeared and a recognizable modern frame had

Robert Campin (1387–1455). Early Flemish painter. The simple moulded frames matched the panelled houses of the merchant class of that time (National Gallery)

developed, consisting of an outer and inner narrow moulding and a broader centre flat. The frame on the 'Portrait of a Girl', Studio of Domenico Ghirlandaio (1449–1494) has a broad flat decorated with a remarkably modern running leaf pattern. This useful and handsome class of frames can still be used with a modern or period finish and is very easy and cheap to make. In the 15th century the centre flat area was often painted in classical volutes, rosettes and the like, or had slightly raised ornament of gesso laid on with a brush.

The latter half of the 16th century was an epoch of prodigious invention and discovery of Shakespeare and Michelangelo and the conquest of Mexico and Peru. Painting and architecture, particularly in Italy, had overcome many obstacles. In Rome and Florence painting and related design became less enterpreneurial and more governed by aesthetic and philosophical theory. Painters were given to elongation of figures and small heads. It became much more secular in subject matter and quite frequently was sexual in subject matter, in an astringent sort of way. 'Leda and the Swan', for instance, was a typical subject.

Colours became more strident with sharp yellows, pinks and

Duccio di Buoninsegna (1260–1319). Madonna triptych. Duccio was the founder of the Sienese school which was partly responsible for the initiation of picture framing (National Gallery)

greens. El Greco, trained in Venice under Titian, was typical, although his favourite framing derived from the late 15th-century style, with a broad centre flat, but unadorned and painted a dark colour, commonly green. Yellow ochre was used to replace gold, possibly to avoid a colour clash. This period is known in English as 'Mannerist' from the Italian 'Gran Maniera'. Tintoretto, the later Michelangelo and above all Parmigianino were exponents of this search for novelty and the extreme gesture of nude figures (*contraposto*). By the end of the 16th century the intimations of baroque rhythms are evident in painting, the ornamental use of the scallop shell, the nautilus (or snail) shell and the half figure, ending up in a foliage pilaster from the groin downwards, became fashionable. In framing, the designs were very varied, heavy architectural invention, forcefully applied predominated, but it could be more restrained.

In the north a generation later, in Protestant Holland and Catholic Antwerp, the two greatest painters, Rembrandt van Rijn (1606–69) and Peter Paul Rubens (1577–1640) still derived, if that is a fair word, from the Mannerist tradition, and their framing was rich and heavy. Shown below is a sketch by Rembrandt for the framing of his 'Anatomy Lesson of Dr. Deyman' (Ryksmuseum) in 1656. This was intended for the Amsterdam Anatomical Theatre, not a private house. Domestic framing or 'gallery framing' in private or even ducal collections was much simpler. The painting of the 'Cognoscenti' (Nat. Gall. London), shows the duality in taste between northern and Italianate fashions in the 1620s.

The painting 'The Guitar Player' (Iveagh Bequest, Kenwood House, London, on page 13) by Vermeer of Delft (1632–75) shows externally and internally two very typically 17th-century frames, one peculiarly Dutch and one more generally used. The real frame is cut in walnut with a variety of wave patterns and highly polished. Ebonizing was also popular. Such severely rectangular frames in decorative woods with subtle textural carving continued in popularity until the 1930s, but they were originally a valiant attempt at native Protestant sensuality, deeply suspicious of Italian Papist exuberance and the 'Jesuit inspired' flamboyance of the Counter Reformation. The frame on the landscape in the painting is ornamented and gilded and has hints of the baroque style to the extent that there is an emphasis on a heavier corner ornament, a device that developed towards the end of the century and became in a looser, more organic way one of the most characteristic features of the more curvacious, more feminine Rococo style by the 1720s. The painter Watteau bridges both styles in frames, but belonged heart and soul to the latter.

First used derogatively, the word 'baroque' is said to derive from the Portuguese for a misshapen pearl, such as were fashionable for miniature sculptures in the guise of jewellery, earrings and the like.

As a style in any of the arts, baroque had a serene certainty, but it had equally a restless waywardness which encouraged a tendency towards surprises, particularly in architecture. It was extremely abstract, although the elements that were distorted were all of classical origin. The extent to which it was the particular expression of the Roman reaction to Protestant Europe is less important than its capacity to adapt to different societies. St. Paul's in London, designed by Sir Christopher Wren (1632–1723) is certainly baroque, but in an austere northern way which seems far removed from the

Rembrandt Van Rijn (1606–69). Rembrandt had two 'Anatomy Lesson' commissions. This is his draft sketch of the frame for 'The Anatomy Lesson of Dr Deyman'; a heavily enshrined painting for the Amsterdam Anatomical Theatre (Ryksmuseum)

'The Guitar Player' by Jan Vermeer (1632–75) in Kenwood House, showing two 17th-century frames. One, outside the painting is characteristically Dutch, while the frame within the painting is more in the French style (Victoria and Albert Museum)

theatrical effulgence of the Piazza Navona in Rome by Bernini (1598–1690), the great master of the style.

In framing, baroque was able to contain many degrees of opulence or simplicity. The pictures on pages 14–17 show an anglo-Dutch frame from Ham House by the Thames, a Spanish baroque frame, and a Grinling Gibbons (1648–1721) from the Victoria & Albert Museum.

The Spanish baroque frame shares with French frames the claim to be the most perfect product of the craft of framing. Its dark background colour and its muted ornament make it one of the great pleasures of the Prado Museum in Madrid. The Velasquez 'Lady with a Fan' (Wallace Collection, London, see page 15) gives a good idea of its sombre sensuality. Ideal for certain portraits, it is a fairly easy frame to build from scratch.

Rococo was a sinuous, curvacious development from baroque, a baroque shorn of its political pretensions and assumption of autocratic power. It was essentially a French style, though of course it spread to many countries, most comfortably in Germany and more superficially (although fashionably) in England. Cabinet-makers like Johnson and Chippendale were responsible for very elaborate rococo picture and glass frames in the 'Chinese' style and the 'Gothic' style, both English.

This example of Anglo-Dutch baroque framing is one of a series in the grand gallery, Ham House, Richmond on Thames, and contains a portrait of Charles I by the studio of Van Dyck (Victoria and Albert Museum)

Most framers and painters were necessarily more cautious than such trendsetters. Hogarth, despite his francophobia, was a rococo painter and his framing was similar. But the rococo frame seems to have persisted in England through the neo-classical phase that followed and through the Regency period.

A drawing by John Constable to his framer in the early 19th century shows how persistent was the style, which survived to merge with its revival in France after the restoration of the monarchy and in early Victorian England.

Following the discovery of the ruins of Herculaneum in the middle of the 18th century, and coinciding with the new style of neo-classical painting, the neo-classical style of framing spread throughout Europe. In effect it consisted of straightened out Rococo with the addition of neo-Roman ornament and moulding details.

French neo-classical was more austere and can be recognized by the emphasis on the cavetto or scoop in the moulding and the ubiquity of pearl beading, (see page 17).

Diego Velasquez (1599–1660). Frames shown in his paintings seem to be mannerist as with Rembrandt, but shortly afterwards this type of frame became characteristically Spanish (Wallace Collection)

The Empire frame became widespread in France at the beginning of the 19th century. A rather severe attenuation of Neo-Classicism, it was best suited to the stark paintings of Jacques Louis David (1748–1825), the prophet of republican severity and rectitude. It is said that vast numbers of frames were destroyed in the revolution for the sake of the gold leaf and many paintings in the Louvre were inappropriately framed in the Empire style. Later in the 19th century the style was introduced into England, when people had overcome their political feelings and wished to flaunt their French taste, a trifle out of date.

The French restoration of the monarchy produced a reversion in taste for the *ancien régime*. Neo-rococo and neo-Louis XIV frames were developed and were manufactured in their hundreds in many countries. A favourite was the oval spandrelled frame.

The later 19th century produced a large new middle class whose parlours demanded decoration like the salons of earlier times. Styles became eclectic, drawn from all periods, rococo, mannerist, 'gothic' and combinations of fancy beyond measure. It is impossible here to give a representative selection of Victorian frames, but some examples are shown on pages 68, 79 and 80.

Dante Gabriel Rossetti (1828–82) the Pre-Raphaelite painter, designed his own frames and was copied by some disciples. He liked flatness and disliked mitred corners, but he also devised various simple but unique mouldings. His colleague Holman Hunt (1827–1910) journeyed around the Levant, painting mosques and scapegoats and designing frames of symbolic significance and at enormous cost.

In the early 20th century, 19th-century styles continued for a few decades, though tending towards greater simplicity. The Matisse framing in the Armory Exhibition (New York, 1913) is minimal in the extreme and this tendency was reinforced by the Bauhaus painters in Germany before the Nazis forced them into exile. But individual painters, Gustav Klimt, Paul Klee and indeed Matisse himself used or adapted ornamental frames of various kinds.

Old paintings have a right to a suitable frame from their own period and generally make more sense that way, but framing will always be a passing fashion for some, with the exercise of aesthetic judgment and experience for the more perceptive.

The Cognocenti. This anonymous painting of a 17th-century picture gallery gives a good idea of contemporary taste. Apart from overcrowding and clothing, little has changed (National Gallery, London)

'Mrs Congrave with her Children' painted by Phillip Renagle (1749–1833), a conversation piece which indicates taste in framing and decor at the end of the 18th century (National Gallery of Ireland)

Now believed to be a forgery, this example is nonetheless typical of Grinling Gibbons (1648–1721), royal woodcarver and colleague of Sir Christopher Wren. He specialised in the realistic use of fruit and wild flower motifs

Tenon saw

Bradawl

Drill

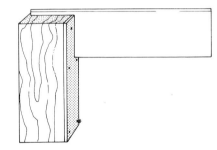

Mitre block

Tri-square

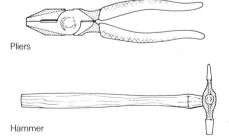

Pliers

Hammer

A BASIC MOULDING AND MITRE CUTTING FOR ALL MOULDINGS

THE PURPOSE of a picture frame is to protect, to isolate the picture, to emphasize it and to acclimatize it to the room in which it hangs. All of these functions are of equal importance and involve various skills, historical interests, imaginative taste and judgment. Do not despair, however, the capacity for many arts and crafts lie latent in many people, otherwise books like this would not be read.

Most frames are rectangular, the occasional exceptions are the round (*tondo*), the octagonal, a passing fashion in 17th-century Holland and the oval and the spandrelled frame. This last type is a decorated rectangular frame with an oval or round picture opening, dating roughly 1800 to 1870.

To make a rectangular frame the following tools are either necessary or extremely useful:
1) a vice to fasten to a sturdy table or bench
2) a tenon saw 12 inches (300 mm) long, 3 inches (75 mm) deep, excluding the back and 12 teeth to the inch (25 mm)
3) a sharp slender bradawl
4) a hand or electric drill with assorted fine bits
5) one of several mitre blocks, metal, wood or plastic
6) a tri square for checking 90° angles
7) pliers
8) a 4-oz (100 g) hammer
9) PVA white wood glue. $\frac{5}{8}$-inch (16 mm): $\frac{3}{4}$-inch (19 mm): 1-inch (25 mm) moulding pins and 1-inch (25-mm), $1\frac{1}{4}$-inch 32-mm), $1\frac{1}{2}$-inch (38-mm) and 2-inch (51-mm) panel pins

All frames are constructed from mouldings, strips of wood, plain or decorated from about $\frac{1}{2}$ inch (12 mm) across the face to 6 inches (150 mm). Here we are mainly concerned with mouldings up to about $2\frac{1}{2}$–3 inches (64–76 mm). Every moulding has an overhang on the side nearest the picture, known as the 'sight' side. The picture or mount slots underneath this overhang, which is called a rebate or a rabbet. All the cuts on a piece of moulding capable of being joined into a frame slope inwards towards this rebate.

Most mouldings are bought ready-made and finished and in a wide variety. Plain, unfinished mouldings can also be bought and stained, textured or waxed to taste. For narrower mouldings this is much cheaper and often better and more individual. Architectural mouldings used by builders can also be adapted to framing, cheaply, and can be given handsome and interesting finishes. Later in this book I will describe the making of ornamental mouldings, cast or copied from old frames or collections, none of which can be bought. Such mouldings as these are usually cheaper to make than the more meretricious machine-stamped mouldings available over the counter.

After the initial preparation of reverse moulds, the results should be much more magnificent and at a fraction of the price. The amount of labour involved is greater, but this is usually a stimulus to the connoisseur or the gifted amateur.

The measurements and precision necessary for assembling a frame is, like taking driving lessons, tedious but unavoidable. I have found when teaching that the soundest beginning is to persuade the student to make a simple moulding mostly from soft, square timber. This behaves well, pins easily, saws easily and instils the whole basis of framing in the mind, cheaply and optimistically. To make a mess of expensive and possibly unsuitable factory-made mouldings at the start can and does cause terminal discouragement.

Buy in any timber shop a 6-foot (2-m) length of one inch-by-one inch (25 × 25-mm) timber (not hardwood), and a corresponding length of $\frac{1}{4}$-inch (6-mm) quadrant. The quadrant is in a harder wood, but no matter. This will make a small, simple frame which can be textured, scumbled, colour-washed or gilded, following advice in a later chapter.

First cut off 6 inches (150 mm) of each, spread a line of white PVA wood glue along the piece of quadrant and press it along a top edge of the piece of one-by-one. This makes a very short piece of very simple moulding. Make two like this if you like, they are for practice only. Allow half an hour for drying in a warm room. It may seem childish to some, but a surprising number of people are slow to grasp how the mitres slant towards the rebate. In this case, the rebate has been formed by the addition of the quadrant piece.

The mitre cutter recommended here, both for beginners and more experienced framers, is the Marples cramp cutter which at a pinch can be used for joining corners, although a separate corner cramp is more flexible for manipulation. It can be screwed to the table or bench, but more conveniently screwed to an 8-inch (203-mm) length of 2 × 1 inch (two-by-one) (50 × 25 mm) which can then be gripped in the vice, which is clamped to the table. In such a cutter, the left-hand clamp is needed for a right-hand mitre cut and vice versa.

Take one of the 6-inch (150-mm) pieces of moulding and set it flatly and squarely in the cramp of the mitre cutter with the rebate away from you and the back of the moulding pressed by the screw pad. The left-hand side of the cutter guides a right-hand mitre and vice versa; this sounds confusing but is instantly obvious. Set the piece of moulding in the left-hand side so that the saw cuts from one end, or a fraction in from the end. Saw smoothly and horizontally until you are through. Remove saw and moulding and look at the back of the latter to check if the profile makes a right angle with the base and top. If the cut slopes outwards, or inwards, the moulding is not lying squarely on the rebate side or on its bottom. This is a common beginner's error and a careful scrutiny before sawing is always worth while. Some mouldings tip forward when tightened too much, particularly narrow ones. Suggestions for avoiding this are given below.

Take any similar piece of squared wood, rebated or not, and practise several more cuts, setting the wood back $\frac{1}{4}$ inch (6 mm) at a time until some confidence is acquired. It might be worth while setting a piece of wood or moulding at a slight angle in the cutter and sawing a mitre. Try also setting a matchstick under the bottom of the wood towards the lock. Examine both cuts, neither will show a clean right angle when viewed from the back.

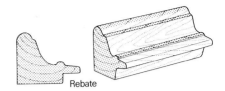

All frames have a rebate in which the picture or glass lies

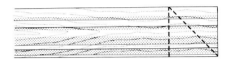

All mitres are the diagonal of an implied square, one side of which is the width of the frame

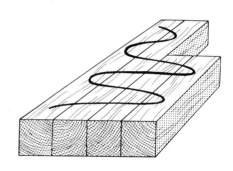

Timber is often not quite square. Assemble the pieces together until they are level and make a mark, denoting the 'face'

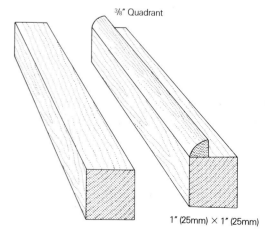

Piece of squared timber with a strip of quadrant timber added to form a rebate

Set the moulding in the mitre cutter, for example for a right-hand cut, with the rebate away from you

Slide in the saw and begin gently and gradually to increase the strokes

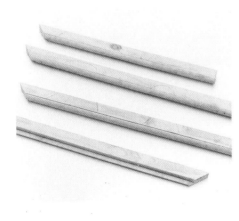

Mitre each side constantly right or left. The cuts always slope inwards from the outside towards the rebate

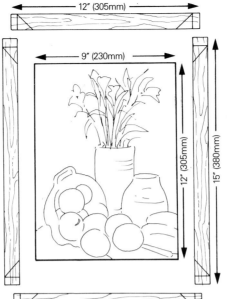

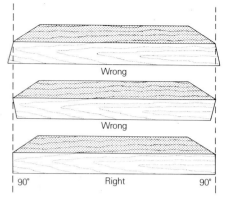

Above: The profile of the mitred moulding should show a right angle at the ends when viewed from the back (outside) of the moulding

Left: Cut off rough lengths a little longer than needed

To make a small, robust frame from the remaining pieces of one-by-one (25 × 25 mm) and ¼-inch (6-mm) quadrant, a size must be chosen from the remaining 5 feet (1·5 m) of timber. The largest convenient size would be to fit a picture 12 × 9 inches (305 × 230 mm).

When measuring for a frame, the length and height of the picture must be measured. In this case it has to be 12 × 9 inches (305 × 230 mm) or less. To each of these measurements must be added twice the width of the moulding. On paper the moulding is 1¼ inches (32 mm) wide but in practice it is less. Soft timber is never the full described size when it is bought 'finished', i.e. planed smooth from the original hairy saw cuts. A piece of finished one-by-one (25 × 25 mm) will be between ¾ inch (19 mm) and ⅞ inch (22 mm) in width and probably not quite square and a smooth piece of two-by-one (50 × 25 mm) could be as little as 1¾ × ¾ inches (44 × 19 mm). Assuming the 12 × 9-inch (305 × 230-mm) measurement, adjustable proportionately, cut two lengths of the one-by-one each measuring 12 + 1 + 1 inches (305 + 25 + 25 mm) plus an extra inch for safety; then cut two lengths measuring 9 + 1 + 1 inches (230 + 25 + 25 mm) and an extra inch; these lengths should be cut square, not mitred. This makes a total of 54 inches (1·37 m), two pieces 15 inches (380 mm) long, and two pieces 12 inches (305 mm) long.

Every mitre angle of 45° is the diagonal of the square of the moulding. From this it can be seen that the outer perimeter is longer than the 'sight' side of the moulding by twice the side of this square, i.e. twice the width of the moulding. Always allow a little extra when cutting.

One-by-one (25 × 25-mm) timber as bought is rarely quite square in cross-section. This can throw corners higher or lower if the cut pieces are accidentally permutated. To avoid this make a wavy pencil line down any side to denote an arbitrary 'face' and keep this side uppermost when assembling the frame.

It is not advisable to cut a mitre from a long length of timber or moulding. It tends to lift slightly in the mitre cutter or block. Better to cut the length into square-ended pieces a little longer than needed (an inch [25 mm] or less if necessary) for each of the four sides. These can be mitred more safely. Cut two 15-inch (380-mm) lengths of one-by-one (25 × 25 mm) (or two-by-one/50 × 25 mm) and glue a strip of ¼-inch (6-mm) quadrant along the edge of the 'face'. Cut the 12-inch (305-mm) sides and glue the quadrant similarly. Dribble a line of white PVA wood glue (Evostic W or Dunlop) on one side of the quadrant and press it tightly onto one side of the one-by-one and press it on firmly along the top edge. If there is a bend in the quadrant as sometimes happens, lightly tap in a ⅝-inch (16-mm) moulding pin at either end, just enough so that they don't fall out. Then offer the piece to the top edge of the timber and partly drive in the pin so that it can be removed with pliers before mitring. Nails must not be allowed to foul saw teeth. The pins are temporary attachments while the glue dries, this takes about a quarter of an hour.

Lay the fully mitred sides back-to-back against the half-mitred corresponding side

When the assembled pieces of moulding are dry, mitre the same end of each of the four pieces, either left or right, but be consistent to save confusion. Take the picture and set it against the inside of the rebate, where the mitre cut has sliced it. Mark the other end with a pencil, still on the back of the rebate, allowing 1/16 inch (2 mm). Allow ⅛ inch (3 mm) for canvas, which is bulky at the corners. Remove the picture and find the point on the face where your pencil line would emerge, assuming it were a very fine pin. This is achieved by continuing the pencil line under the overhang of the rebate and across its top on the face, back as far as the depth of the rebate. Make a small dot at the end of the pencil line, set the moulding in the mitre cutter so that the saw lies across the dot and cuts through it. The mitre cut will automatically travel from farther out on the outside of the moulding to farther in on the 'sight' side. Cut a long and a short side like this. The two corresponding opposite sides are more easily marked. Set one of the completely cut pieces on a level surface and one of the half-cut pieces by it back-to-back. Mark the unfinished piece on the back, set it in the mitre cutter and adjust until the saw lies on the top of the line. The cut should travel down the line, obliterating it. Treat both unfinished pieces similarly and set opposite sides back-to-back to test for equal size. Should some error of judgment have been made, it can be remedied by using a shooting board and plane, which will be described at the end of this chapter. It is a nuisance however, and the reader should follow these instructions carefully to avoid having to do this.

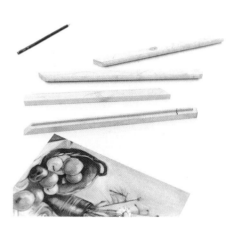

Extend the pencilling over the rebate edge to above the back (inside) of the rebate

The four mouldings must now be joined and the most convenient way to do this is first to join two different lengths and then join them together to form a rectangle. The short leg of an L-joint can face to the left or the right. It does not matter which way, but both L-shaped pieces must face in the same direction. These will join correctly together. Try the unjoined pieces before glueing and nailing, and at some point in permutating them, you will see why. Hardwood needs to be drilled with a narrow bradawl, a hand drill or an electric drill. For soft wood, a shallow start with a bradawl is enough to set the pin and the hammering is light.

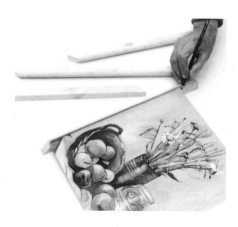

Lay the picture on the inside of the rebate from the mitre cut. Pencil the open end with a slight allowance

Pins should be driven at a distance in from the end so that the pin pierces the mitre cut about half way through its area. The pin length is determined by the necessity to penetrate the other side of the corner for about half of its length. After restoring perhaps hundreds of old frames, one hundred to two hundred years old, I realize that

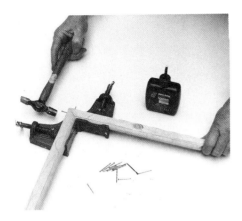

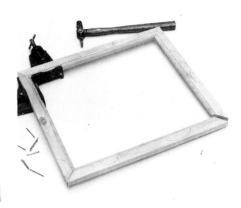

Glue the ends of two unequal sides, place them in the corner cramp, and hammer in pins

The two identical shapes, glued, pinned and removed from the cramp

The two L-shapes glued, replaced in the cramp and pinned

The last unjoined corner is glued, tightened into the cramp and pinned

The assembled frame is left flat to dry, awaiting finishing

Test the picture for size in case adjustment is needed

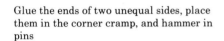

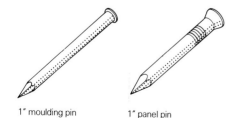

1″ moulding pin   1″ panel pin

two pins per corner are better than one. In old frames the wood shrinks, separating the mitred corners, leaving a gap of $\frac{1}{8}$ inch (3 mm) to $\frac{1}{4}$ inch (6 mm) at times, yet the frame itself, apart from this and broken ornament, is often quite sturdy and safe. But it is fair to say that many framers use only one pin, or two on one side, for a deep frame.

Set the four mouldings together to form a rectangle on a flat surface and mark the pin hole position with a pencil. On any given corner the hole should be up or down slightly on either side so as to avoid the pins hitting. If the moulding is of a hard brittle wood, as is often the case these days, set each piece lightly in a vice, sight side downwards, and drill through at the pencil point, using a drill slightly narrower than the pin, and at the slight angle indicated on page 26. This tightens better than drilling straight and affords a better angle for hitting with the hammer, thus reducing the mischance of a bent pin. If a pin bends halfway in, pull it out with pliers, gripping with the wire cutter and levering.

Buy a selection of a few ounces each of moulding pins $\frac{5}{8}$-inch (16-mm), $\frac{1}{4}$-inch (6-mm) and 1-inch (25-mm), and for heavier frames panel pins 1-inch (25-mm), 1¼-inch (32-mm), 1½-inch (38-mm) and 2-inch (50-mm). Only common sense and the size and bulk of the moulding will determine which to use.

In this case, use a 1-inch (25-mm) panel pin, thicker than a 1-inch (25-mm) moulding pin and able to grip harder in soft wood. Set a long and short piece in a corner cramp with one side only of the mitre, covered in PVA wood glue. It is possible to use the Marples mitre cutter to grip the mouldings, but it is less flexible to use than a separate corner cramp and more awkward for hammer access. Drive in a 1-inch (25-mm) panel pin on both sides of the corner and remove the joined pieces. Join the other two pieces, but copy the same L-junction, whether its leg turns left or right. If the first L has a right leg, so must the second and vice versa. Now apply glue to two cuts on one L-join, and assemble the two sections in a corner cramp. Pin one side, remove the joined corner and set in the last unjoined one and drive in the last two pins. Remove the joined frame and leave flat for a couple of hours for the glue to dry, though further work can be done on its surface by taking care and not imposing a strain on the wet joints.

The result will be a very simple and unexciting raw wooden frame in either one-by-one (25 × 25-mm) timber or two-by-one (50 × 25 mm), whichever is chosen. It is a comparatively simple and agreeable

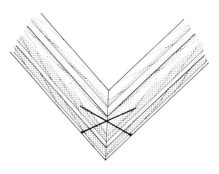

After glueing, the pins are driven in at the angle shown to give a tangle hold

The basic frame before and after finishing with gesso

task to enrich this frame in various textures, tones, colour washes, silver or gold both to transform it and to learn fundamental techniques in the process. These will be described in Chapter 5. The main purpose of making such a basic frame, however, is to combine a number of techniques without much expense or frustration. I have used it in teaching for many years and found it very effective.

All made-up mouldings are cut and joined in the manner described above, though narrower mouldings are always more difficult to handle. A common mistake is to use too narrow a moulding for a large area of glass. The tiny contact points at the corners are not very strong and disasters happen after a year or two in a dry atmosphere. In general, there seems to be a widespread puritan fear of any generosity in frame dimensions. The frame should be appropriate, neither simple nor elaborate.

Most beginners and many more experienced framers will expect to use factory-made mouldings. Some are well designed, particularly if they are purchased from a good stockist, but many on sale are 'plastic' and meretricious.

Clockwise from top left: A plastic Stanley mitre block, a wooden mitre block, and a Marples mitre guide operated from the side on which the screws are situated

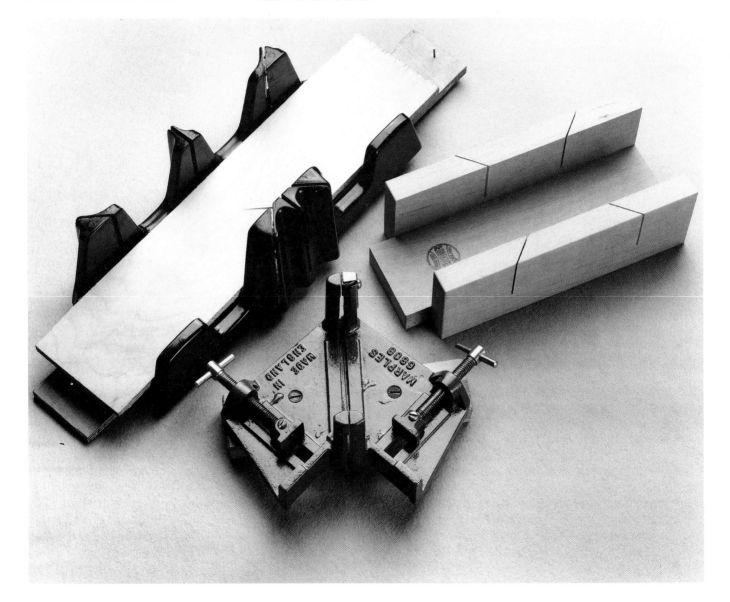

Choice is a matter of judgment, taking account of colour, texture and width. Offensive and garish 'gold' finishes can be stippled with brown gouache in size as described elsewhere and wax polished. Bruised corners can be filled with tinted wax or warmed wax crayons of appropriate colour. Wax gold amalgam can be used as a filler and polished when dried hard.

There are techniques for cutting and joining mouldings other than those just described. A U-shaped wooden mitre-block can be used, holding the moulding against the far wall of the trough. Wooden mitre blocks are the oldest, and have been used for at least five centuries. They are quite satisfactory, provided you keep a strong grip to keep the length of moulding from jumping. The Stanley tool manufacturers make a plastic mitre block based on the wooden one. It needs the addition of a flat piece of wood into which the saw teeth can cut after passing through the moulding, and also a base strip with a piece of two-by-one (50×25-mm) to form a T-structure to fit in a vice. The saw slots are rather loose, perhaps due to the plastic casting methods, but it is possible to glue a strip of mounting board inside

A wide variety of commercially made mouldings is available in many different finishes and sizes

The Ulna Variable cutter is effective and versatile, but a little expensive

Gripping angles vary according to taste, and practice is needed

them with a contact adhesive. These last longer than might be expected and can be quickly replaced. It will take mouldings of nearly 4 inches (100 mm) in width.

The Jointmaster cutter is made of metal and cuts a variety of carpentry joints as well as mitres. The mouldings are held by an ingenious system of nylon pegs and a wooden wedge. It cuts up to 2-inch (51-mm) mouldings. For intense use, for any size of moulding, the Ulna Variable mitre cutter with saw is very effective, but it is much more expensive than the others mentioned here. The guillotine is also very expensive and not very effective for richly decorated mouldings. It is generally used by jobbing framers who tend to use factory-made mouldings from $\frac{1}{2}$-inch (12-mm) to 2 inches (51 mm) in width. It needs mentioning but its use is outside the scope of this book.

There are two other means for joining mitred corners which need consideration: joining in a vice and with an Elwood wire cramp. Joining with a vice needs practice, beginning with two pieces of unrelated one-by-one (25×25 mm) and graduating to narrower or more complex mouldings. Quite short pieces can be used for experience. First drill the two corner cuts, so that the pins can be driven through so that they barely pierce the far side. Set one longer length in a vice as shown on page 26. Smear white wood glue on one side, but not so much as to squash out onto the face. If this should happen, wipe with a damp cloth within a few minutes. Offer the mitred end of the short piece to the mitred end protruding from the vice but

Above: 'Shooting' is the controlled planing of a mitre cut on a guiding board or device

Card 'stops' glued on to the face of an electric plane to distance it from the shooting board

slightly offset as shown on page 26, with the mitred point of the hand-held piece up by about $\frac{1}{16}$ inch (1·6 mm) from the outer corner. This amount varies according to the size of the moulding.

The act of hammering in the first pin drives the hand-held piece into alignment. Make two L-joints as before and join them together, holding the appropriate side in the vice. It will not come right the first or second time, but it is worth persevering.

The Elwood cramp is a device, useful for large frames whereby a wire cable passes through three corner fittings and is joined to a tightening device on the fourth corner. Pins can be driven into three corners, but the device must be removed before the last corner can be pinned, hand-held, lying flat on the bench.

In all pin driving, the last $\frac{1}{8}$-inch (3 mm) should be driven below the wood surface with a punch. In finished mouldings this can be filled with a scrap of melted wax crayon, or a wood filler tinted with paint.

Since at least the 18th century a device called a shooting board has been employed to shave the end of a mitred cut with a plane. The cut mitre can be held in this to be accurately shaved very thinly to shorten the moulding slightly or correct a bad cut; the merest shaving which may need repeating several times to remove $\frac{1}{10}$ inch (2·5 mm). Page 27 shows one in action, with two stopping blocks forming a 40° angle with each other. Only one is used at a time depending on whether a left- or right-hand mitre cut is being shaved. Mitre shooting boards are still used and can be bought, but hand electric planes can be adapted to them as shown on page 27. Electric hand planes vary in contour, so the adaptation has to be worked out for different models. In effect it consists in glueing strips of mounting board onto the plane face to distance it from the step of the shooting board a little, to avoid planing it away. The mitre cut is held a fraction further out from the step than the thickness of the strips of mounting board stops glued to the plane face. Four or five slices with the electric plane will remove up to $\frac{1}{4}$ inch (6 mm) rapidly and cleanly, the non-electric jack plane is apt to jerk in inexperienced hands.

MOUNT CUTTING

MOUNT CUTTING came into practice in the middle of the 19th century as a means of protecting and stretching drawings, water-colours, prints, engravings, lithographs and so forth. Apparently evolved from the printer's margin, it has the same function of setting the comparative lightness of the image in a neutral area of plain tone, frequently but not universally contained in a narrow unemphatic frame. The totality of mount and frame constitutes the setting on which the picture depends.

The mount is therefore something more than a sheet of card with a hole in the middle, although that is the primary consideration here.

Mounting (or matting) board is made from wood pulp faced with paper and is chemically treated to minimize an acid attack on the picture paper. On no account should strawboard be used or the picture paper will deteriorate extremely quickly. Sizes of board are from Trimmed Royal ($24 \times 19\frac{1}{2}$ inches/610×495 mm) to Antiquarian (54×36 inches/1370×915 mm) untrimmed, but the most common, sold by most art shops, is Trimmed Imperial (22×32 inches/600×810 mm).

The thickness of a board is reckoned in 'sheets': 4 sheet to 10 sheet. Most art shops seem to be confined to 4 sheet, though some have 6 sheet. The thicker the board the wider the bevelled window cut, and sometimes this deeper recession is desirable. 4 sheet is enough to get by on if you cannot find a better retailer, though it is often light.

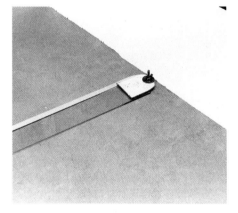

A soft fibre board with a swivelling straight edge. A glass strip is both cheap and effective

The mount can be cut with a sharp knife (preferably a Stanley knife with a new blade). This requires several hours' patient practice on a couple of sheets of card, but is worth it. There are however several mount-cutting tools available, but I have found that the 'Dexter' is by far the best, though it needs the addition of a simple home-made distance gauge. A tool like the Dexter is merely a sliding metal block which holds a sharp blade at a 45° angle. The rest of the work has to be done by its user. But it does take the pain out of the process, particularly for beginners, and for a long time after.

Estimating the width of the margin visually

A sheet of builder's fibre board is needed as a cutting base, a straight edge and a 45°, 45°, 90° set-square. Most framing books recommend a 3-foot (91-cm) bevelled steel straight edge, but I have found that this is not necessary, they are very expensive and not easy to buy. I use a strip of window glass about $2\frac{1}{2}$ inches (64 mm) wide. Fix a flat piece of plywood with a hole in it to one end of this, cement it on with an epoxy resin. This is fixed to swing from one side of the piece of fibre board with a small bolt, washer and butterfly nut; this is much easier to hold rigidly when cutting, where any movement of the straight edge can be disastrous. The leading edge of the glass strip should be rubbed smooth with a carborundum stone to remove sharp grit, the rest can be sellotaped over the edge.

Choose the colour of your mount card carefully. Take your picture to the art shop and hope for imaginative inspiration. Space does not permit discussion of relating the colour of the mount to the picture and the frame, particularly because there are no set rules involved. It can only be said here, rather cryptically that there is a time for conservatism and a time for daring.

1. Lay the card colour up on a clean table covered with old newspapers.
2. Put the picture at one corner and move it up an imaginary diagonal line until a margin that looks right shows on two sides. It can be narrow or wide. Some pictures need more isolation than others. Very small pictures often need proportionately larger mounts to add importance, as with frames.
3. Take a pair of compasses (the cheaper kind used in schools with a length of pencil attached will do). Set these to the width of the chosen margin and mark that distance on a piece of card or paper in case the compasses move in later handling.
4. Turn the mount board face downwards and lay the picture in approximately the same position as before.
5. Adjust the two available margins from the compasses and, laying its points one at a time on both the inward sides, mark outwards to obtain a small pencilled arc from each to denote the limits of the mount.

Top left: Gauging the width of the mount with a pair of compasses

Top right: Cutting off the surplus mounting board from the sheet

Above left: Pricking a hole from the back of the card where the compass pencil lines join

Above right: The back of the card showing four pin pricks denoting the limits of the mount aperture

Above: Cutting the first side of the mount with a Stanley knife at a 45° angle to the surface on the front of the card in order to achieve a bevelled cut

Above right: Ready to cut the first side of the mount with a Dexter cutter with the home-made distance gauge in position. In both cases the straight edge is in from the prick by the extent of the black on the distance gauge

6. Without moving the picture (or readjusting it with compasses if it has moved) extend the compasses by about a $\frac{1}{4}$ inch (6 mm) (more or less is a matter of necessity or judgment) into the margins of the picture. The 'window' must be smaller than the picture, or the amount of picture that has been chosen to expose.

7. Mark the width of the newly increased compass spread for reference in case it moves, and lay it aside for a few moments.

8. Take the set square and align it as shown, and pencil a line through first one arc and then the other. Continue these lines until they join. This enclosed rectangular area is the size of your mount and must be cut from the complete sheet of mount board. If several relatively small mounts are needed, test the pictures for economic positioning.

9. Tighten the wing nut that holds the strip of glass on the cutting bed of fibre board so that it admits the sheet of mount board firmly but not too tightly.

10. Align the cutting edge along your first pencil mark and cut firmly and smoothly towards you, at a 90° angle, with a sharp Stanley knife or something similar. If you are unfamiliar with cutting, sacrifice a strip of your board and make practice cuts until it comes cleanly. When satisfied, cut along both pencil lines, releasing the desired rectangle of mount board. It should and must be a perfect rectangle. Check with a set square and trim when necessary.

11. Take your pair of compasses, already set to give the margins and a little extra to cover the edge of the picture, lay the point against the top of the right-hand edge of the board, and with the compasses held nearly upright, inclining slightly towards you and the pencil the chosen distance in on the back of the board, draw it evenly towards you. Make sure that the table on which the mount board lies is smooth, or the compass point will jump. A pencil line will have been made on the mount board of the exact width needed. Do this on all four sides. The area inside these lines must be removed and since you are working on the back of the board marks do not matter.

The inside piece of card is removed from the mount after cutting. Always leave the Dexter cutter upside down after use, to avoid damaging the blade tip

12. Now take a pin and prick through the board just inside the juncture of the four pencil lines. The pricks must be small but clearly visible on the face side.

13. Turn the board face side up and align any two pin pricks with the right-hand or cutting edge of the glass straight-edge. If you have mastered hand-cutting with a knife, cut along the glass from pin hole to pin hole, holding the knife at a 45° angle. Proceed clockwise around the card, taking care not to overshoot the pin pricks at each corner. If a bevelled steel straight-edge is used, the bevel should be on the left of the steel, just touching two pin pricks.

This, like all hand-cutting, requires diligent practice and rehearsal. Do not expect it to come quickly. If the picture is a topographical print, an engraving or a lithograph, there is a convention that the lower margin of the mount should be deeper than the other three. With a water-colour or anything similar this looks silly, particularly with a coloured mount. In marking up the compasses, do the lower margin first and, holding the picture in position with the spare hand, lift the lower edge of the picture and run the compasses along. Then readjust the compasses for the narrower sides.

Apart from very small graphic work inset in large mounts, this convention has little optical validity, since the 18th century when prints were hung like stamps in an album from cornice to wainscote. Watercolours from Girtin, Turner and Bovington onwards began with the English Regency and through much of the 19th century were framed like small oils. A mount, particularly a coloured one, reads as part of the general framing and, it seems to me, should be treated without regard to the convention in question. Topographical wash drawings in pale tones often improve with line and wash mounts, but with more vigorous colouring this would be irritatingly fussy and distracting. Coloured prints on paper are mostly derived from oil paintings and are best framed as such, pasted on board and given a coat of picture varnish.

To use a Dexter mount-cutting tool effectively a small distance gauge of card must be made. Cut a strip of mount board about $3\frac{1}{2}$ inches (90 mm) long by $\frac{1}{2}$ inch (12 mm) wide. The ends should be square. Set one end against a straight-edge (a strip of glass, for instance) and set the sliding edge of the Dexter tool (left-hand side) against the same part of the straight-edge so that the blade pierces the strip of card. Rule a line across this tiny cut and blacken in the area towards the end as shown. The width of this easily read black rectangle can be used to align the straight-edge on the mount card a constant distance in from the pin holes in a couple of seconds as shown.

14. To cut the mount, as with a knife by hand, lay the card on the cutting board finished side up, and swing the glass straight-edge approximately the width of the black marker in from the line implied by any two consecutive pin pricks. Check that the blade pierces the card and protrudes about $\frac{1}{32}$ inch (1 mm) and screw it tightly.

15. Holding the tool in a south-north direction, since the cutting is done away from you, set it so that the blade adequately pierces the board just a fraction to the south-east of the pin prick. Swing the pivoted straight-edge until it lies along the inside or sliding edge of the Dexter tool, touching it snugly.

16. Set the card distance gauge from the farther pin prick to the straight-edge, which may need a little readjusting.

17. Place your hand on the tool and push gently and firmly away from

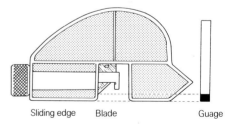

Sliding edge   Blade   Guage

The underneath of a Dexter cutter showing the distance between the blade tip and the edge that runs along the straight edge. Cutting from the back of the card is hazardous as it can result in a rough finish

you, slowing down as you near the farther pin prick and looking into the chimney where the blade can be seen until it fractionally crosses the pin prick.

18. Turn the board around clockwise and start again with the straight-edge, the tool and the distance gauge and cut the second side, and so on. Always keep a firm pressure on the tool, as with a knife, and hold the free end of the straight-edge firmly with the free hand.

It looks very complicated spelled out in words, but it only takes about fifteen minutes.

A few practice runs on a spare piece of board will quickly put flesh on the bones of theory. If the centre of the mount window does not come away with a sharp tap, the corners may need releasing with a sharp knife, held at the appropriate angle.

It should be noticed that in the entire process of measuring a picture, estimating and cutting a mount, it has not been necessary to use a ruler. The complications that flow from double or treble measurements, adding and subtracting and increasing the field of error, are avoided. It does assume the physical presence of the picture, but this should always be the case. A costume designer must have physical reference to age, sex and occasion, and similar considerations apply to pictures and paintings.

The art of mounting (or matting) a picture involves complex matters of judgment and aesthetic choice. Latent capacities in both of these are best extended by visiting private galleries and the better group exhibitions. National collections sometimes tend to be very conservative.

White board is usually more brilliant than the white paper of a print or drawing, and a light ivory may prove more flattering. While all aesthetic rules need to be broken at times, in general a mount, or a

frame for that matter, may well echo a colour in the picture, but not in the same tone. A dominant blue in a watercolour is better matched by a blue-grey board than a blue one. Heavy drawings or woodcuts with large areas of white often look well with a charcoal brown board. All the greys are useful, warm or cold (a touch of yellow or blue). Before deciding on a cream mount, for instance, give a thought to one of the light greys which sometimes look both restful and striking.

Black should be used sparingly, though it can be very enhancing at times. Remember that the colour of a board lies in a thin sheet of paper pasted over it. The darker colours, brown, black, dark green, tend to tear slightly if the cutting blade is not surgically sharp. Occasionally a 'rogue' board occurs in which the colour paper is not fully united to the board. Discard all such.

The preceding instructions were concerned purely with measuring and cutting the card, a difficult enough task for a beginner. But there are at least six sub-species in the mounting category which need some comment.

A *double mount* consists of two window openings, the inner one smaller than the outer one, and usually of a different colour or tone. First the outer limits are defined and cut, and then the precise positioning of the inner mount. Both mounts are then cut with great care for slight variations in parallel will show up badly.

The *lining of mounts* with the addition of bands of colour wash or gold is really a piece of period pastiche and it seems to me that it should be limited to a water-colour style common in the *belle époque* or topographical prints of the same period or whenever it is thought appropriate to suggest the *fin de siècle* or the turn of the century.

The lining is traditionally done with suitable drawing nibs from an art shop and Indian ink, though many will find modern waterproof

A variety of samples of lining and colouring

A double mount consists of an inner and outer mount of different tone or colour, joined as one. It gives extra emphasis when needed

fibre pens more convenient, providing they are blot proof. Gold pens of variable thickness can sometimes replace the traditional gummed gold paper that needs careful cutting and licking. They are also easier to buy. Gold gummed paper in sheets can be bought in specialist framing suppliers. Strips of the required width are cut with a knife and straight-edge. The effect is shinier and more metallic than a gold pen, but this is a matter of judgment. It can throw a picture out of phase if overused or be used where it is downright unsuitable.

The dark lines enclosing a wash-coloured strip should be drawn lightly in pencil, which are then drawn again in ink after the wash has been applied. The wash is thin water-colour, wet and fluid and applied with as few pauses as possible with a suitable sable brush. It helps to wet the area with clear water first. All such efforts should be tested on card scraps and beginners should do several hours' practice until intimations of certainty begin to show.

A simple gauge can be made from a piece of card to mark pencil dots on the four corners of the window which can be joined with ruled lines in any number or sequence of separation needed. Cut a rectangle of card, about 6 inches (150 mm) long by 2 inches (50 mm) wide and cut a 45° angle at one end, with a 45° set-square. Mark off the hypotenuse of this implied triangle in eighths of an inch (3-mm sections), or whatever seems suitable. Do this on both sides of the card. Lay the gauge along any side of the window on the margin and mark the desired points lightly with a pencil. Do this on all corners, as shown, according to the chosen spacing. Join the appropriate pencil points with a black or gold fibre pen, or ink if preferred, but be very careful at the point where the lines join at an angle. This should be practised, as it demands some finesse. Make a note, in galleries or old print shops, of the possible variations. Lining can easily be overdone and frequently has been in the past. As little as a single pencil line can serve to emphasize and sharpen a black-and-white photograph.

A *covered mount* is a means for attaining a richer, more exotic texture and colour. By this I do not mean Whistler peacocks or Sung dragons, but for instance a mount covered in thin raw silk for a Chinese rice-paper painting, enclosed by a carved ivory frame. Or perhaps a coarse, dark brown linen-covered mount for an emphatic woodcut. The tint of fabric can be bought, or dyed, depending on opportunity, and cut to size about 1 inch (25 mm) larger than the mount. Lay the mount on the ironed fabric and paste the outer edges over stretching by hand and glueing with a latex milk such as Copydex or PVA. Make two diagonals in the window and cut them with a sharp knife to within $\frac{1}{10}$ inch (2·5 mm) of the corners, (see illustration). Cut off the surplus indicated by dots, fold over the margins and glue, stretching slightly. Lay under a weighted board for half an hour.

Coloured mounting boards can be bought, but the palette is limited, particularly in the 'pastel' register. It is very difficult to paint mounting board evenly. Brush work always shows and distracts and sprays don't seem to be effective either. The only means that I ever devised successfully is done with flat, matt white (or light coloured) emulsion paint, as for walls and ceilings. Tint this to the desired colour, with gouache or poster colours, which are water-based. Make enough for two coats, thinning slightly since the additions will make it rather heavy. Paint a coat on the uncut board with a good 1-inch (25-mm) round hog brush and allow to dry, which will take half to one hour, depending on temperature. Stipple the second coat evenly and methodically over the first coat, dabbing the hog brush down vertically, like a hairy hammer moving over the card. This will dry to a very fine texture, not unlike certain water-colour papers, and leave a pleasing and hopefully desired tone and colour, not available from commercial manufacturers.

Textured mounts can be in the natural pleasing off-white of the gesso which is used to give the texture or any light tone of colour wash which can be used over the gesso texture, leaving a great deal of white on the highlights of the ridges of the texture, and giving a pleasing 'pointilliste' effect, which can present the painting in a flattering way. Gesso, which is the Italian for 'plaster', will be described later. It is in one form or another a fundamental material in classical framing, and will be found as a white layer under all gilded frames. Properly made, it is stable, lasts for centuries and was the only ground used in 15th-century panel paintings. Badly made, it can crack or flake. A discerning minority of painters today regard it highly as a ground and it is commonly used for tempera painting.

To texture a mount, do not cut the window until afterwards. First size the card with rabbit size, which will be described later, and when dry, paint a coat of gesso over the surface and allow to dry. The choice of texture is a matter of experience; it takes time to judge accurately how a surface will appear when it is deliberately roughened, streaked, scratched or stippled, and how these efforts will look if left as they are or given a wash of colour to any particular depth of tone or hue. Only experiment will broaden this judgment, but to anyone with any interest in painting, the experiments will be both pleasurable and rewarding.

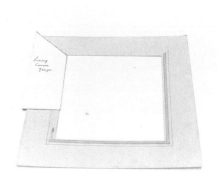

A card gauge which is moved from corner to corner to measure pencil dots which are then joined with a ruler to make the lines

Painting a wash strip between pencilled lines. These lines are later inked

Far left: Samples of mount lining, seen here with a period wash drawing

Left: An abstract expressionist wash drawing with a canvas covered mount

Below: A topographical engraving showing a lined mount

A flat textured frame and textured mount in different colours, contrasting an Indian enamel picture on copper

Gesso texturing can be used not only on mounts, but just as effectively on wood, plain mouldings or parts of mouldings, and hardly ever fails to make the surface more interesting, without interfering with the painting. With acquired deftness it is possible to simulate, cheaply but durably, the feeling of linen, fossilized stone, bronze, copper in any key, high or low as might be thought supportive and flattering. These latter are the only criteria, in equal measure.

Tools are needed, but they need to be acquired or made as often as not, rather than bought. Plastic nail brushes, plastic throwaway toothbrushes or the coarser plastic scrubbing brushes are excellent. They can be sawn or cut into small sections to suit easy handling. One of my best texturing tools is a tiny plastic hairbrush from a doll's toilet set, coaxed by a student from a small girl.

An interesting effect can be obtained by painting on a second coat of gesso on the mount board, having previously sized it and given it one coat of gesso. Paint a rich coat of gesso on one side of the mount, overlapping two corners (see illustration). Wait a few moments for the gesso to gel, and firmly score it with a piece of plastic nail brush or whatever, in any suitable way. Sloping the strokes to the corner is effective, but so is a fish scale pattern of overlapping half-circles. If the gesso dries too much, quickly slap on some more on the half-dried area and proceed right round the margins of the board. The part in the centre which is yet to be cut out can be left bare, but generously overlap its edges. If the lines begin to join up after scratching, the fresh gesso is still too liquid so wait a further thirty seconds.

The scratched (*sgraffito*) lines need not, and indeed should not be exactly uniform. Strive for a general effect as in painting. Leave it to dry for an hour and a colour wash can be applied if needed. Colour washes are in this instance best made from a dab of gouache colour in a small warmed saucer of thin rabbit glue, a transparent tempera. Test out the strength on white paper and thin further or deepen as needed. Spread a generous brushful on some newsprint and dry it, the lettering should be legible. Using a good large hog brush, paint it on quickly, without stopping until the entire surface is covered, and leave to dry. Any lingering will soften the gesso and produce a ghastly mud. Indeed the whole process should be done with speed and

Texturing a mount with a plastic nailbrush in wet gesso

Mount

Textured surface

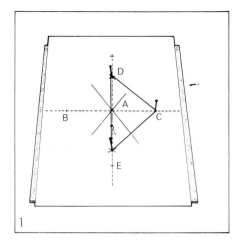

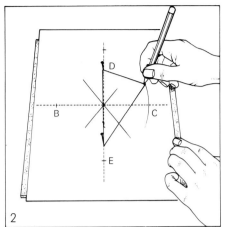

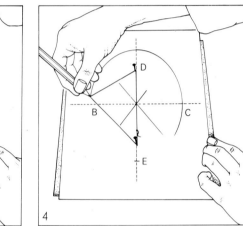

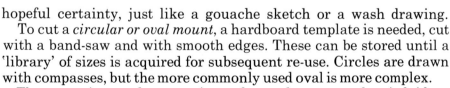

The process of drawing an oval of predetermined size

Top left: Thread the loop around the located pins

Top right: A pencil replaces the pin and the arc then follows the confining thread loop

Bottom left: Continuing the oval contour

Bottom right: The oval half completed.

hopeful certainty, just like a gouache sketch or a wash drawing.

To cut a *circular or oval mount*, a hardboard template is needed, cut with a band-saw and with smooth edges. These can be stored until a 'library' of sizes is acquired for subsequent re-use. Circles are drawn with compasses, but the more commonly used oval is more complex.

The mounting card, cut to size and exactly rectangular, is laid on the cutting board and the centre point established by getting the crossing point of the two diagonals with a ruler. Only pencil the central 'x' of the two crossing lines (see illustration). Using a set-square on one side and a ruler passing through A, tick off half the width of the desired oval with a pair of compasses at points B and C. In a similar way, setting the compasses at half the height of the oval, tick off D and E. With the compasses still set at half the height, set the point at C and describe a short piece of arc above and below A. Set the compasses from B and describe two similar arcs cutting the first two. At the point where these arcs cross, lightly hammer in two 1-inch (25-mm) moulding pins, through the mounting board and securely into the cutting board. Drive a similar moulding pin into point C. Tie a loop of cotton lightly around the base of the three pins, but without any slack. If the knot is fixed with a blob of quick-drying cement it will keep them from slipping. Remove the pin C and substitute a pencil, and allow it to follow its tethered path around the board. The result will be an oval of predetermined size and proportion, wide or narrow, as illustrated.

Right: Two enamel paintings with textured mounts in mid-Victorian and fin de Siècle Japanese styles

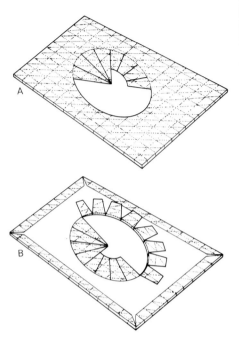

Many oval mounts were covered in silks, velours and linens. The cloth is cut and applied as shown above

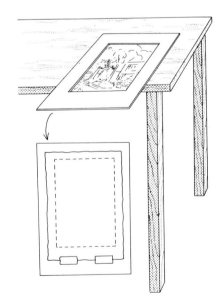

Aligning the print in the mount and, on the back, the initial fixing with gummed tape

It is difficult to cut an oval by hand, but it is possible. A Dexter cutter will do the job, but a template in hardboard must be cut, smaller than the desired oval by the width of the mark on the card gauge. The whole cutting board with the lightly pinned mounting card needs to be revolved during parts of the cutting, particularly at top and bottom and the template, which needs to be pinned down through to the cutting board, rakes the place of a straight-edge. Most frequently an oval mount is needed for a period picture or vignetted photograph, and can be coevered with a fabric, usually an exotic one like velvet. In this case a non-bevelled cut will serve, and a little uncertainty around the edge will not show. The covering of an oval mount is similar to a rectangular one except for the inside lapover of the fabric, which should be as shown.

Papers can be pasted to mounting boards to obtain certain subtle effects of texture or even colour. This can be done as with a fabric. Many papers stretch when wet and subsequently shrink, which bows the mounting board, and a counter paper is needed on the back to even out the stresses. After pasting with a flour or cold water paste, the card should be placed under a board with a weight on top. Good paper shops sell a variety of imitation and real hand-made papers which can be very attractive. Modern spray-on paper adhesives in aerosols can be bought. The particular directions should be followed or adapted. Beginners should not expect instant results. Tricks can be taught but confidence and style come more slowly.

To make an even flour paste, shake a tablespoon of white flour to cover the bottom of a small saucepan and trickle in two tablespoons of cold water, stirring with a hog brush into a smooth cream without lumps. Now add eight tablespoons (120 ml) of cold water, mix, and stir with the brush over a low flame until it has bubbled for about 30 seconds. A few drops of any phenolic antiseptic or half a teaspoon (2·5 ml) of boracic acid crystals added before heating inhibits fungus growth in the event of later humidity.

When taping a paper picture to finished mount, never use a self-sticking tape. These behave disastrously after a few years, and Sellotape is catastrophic. Always use gummed paper tape that needs wetting. This will do no harm to the paper of the painting and is very strong. Even after fifty years it can be removed, by brushing it with water, waiting a few minutes and peeling it off.

Water-colours, usually uneven from the washes, often need a gentle damping on the back with a wrung-out sponge, but never too wet. After fixing the result will sag like a sail in a doldrum, but will tauten and shrink in drying.

To align the picture to the mount window, avoid a ruler whenever possible. Lay the picture over the edge of the table by a few inches and position the mount on top of it. Very fine visual adjustments can be made. Then, holding the picture and mount steady with a spread hand, stick two postage stamp pieces of gummed tape underneath on either side of the base of the back of the picture and onto the back of the card. You have to bend down to see what is happening. Wait ten seconds and turn the board over.

Stick an overlapping strip of gummed paper all round, from one side to its opposite, and attempting to stretch slightly. If it goes wrong, paint the gummed strip with clean water, wait a few moments and it will peel away. Most synthetic tapes or adhesives tear the paper on attempting to remove them.

Competent mounting can be learned in about twelve hours and as many again to gain experience. It is a subtle business in which the cutting and preparation of the mount are the easiest part. Imagination can take over when confidence disolves its constraints.

Aligning the print visually and securing with gummed tabs

Print and mount face down showing the gummed tabs

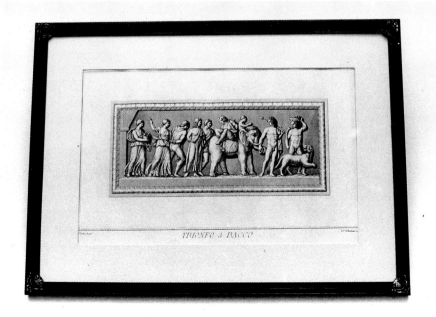

Gummed paper tape securing the print to the mount

Left: A mid-18th-century engraving mounted and framed in a discrete period style for library or study

REPRODUCING FROM ANTIQUE MOULDINGS

I HAVE ALREADY mentioned how cast ornament on frames, altarpieces and other objects were described by Cennini in the 15th century and how the practice became more general and more sophisticated in the last quarter of the 18th century in France and spread elsewhere, since Paris was the centre of fashion and excellence. These methods are still used by the dwindling number of bespoke framemakers today in many countries.

There is a widespread misunderstanding among picture dealers, antique dealers and collectors about cast frames. Each being equal in design and appearance, a carved frame is more desirable, but not all that much. In any case, each is very rarely equal in design. In museums and national collections carved and cast frames hang together and very few people can tell the difference. The main reason that many antique dealers rate cast frames lower is that they have some difficulty repairing them. Either they cannot get the skilled labour or do not want the expense or trouble; probably a mixture of both. I hope to show in a later chapter how anyone with ten intelligent fingers can restore many frames from a few fragments adhering to the wood. The only question is to what extent it is worth while.

The search for frames from which moulds can be taken is a chore. They can be borrowed from friends, a process that takes time after the word has got out that they are needed. Old and severely damaged frames can be bought cheaply. It is a mystery to me why people try to sell them, since without the expertize and labour they are valueless.

Deals can be done with dealers. A loan of a frame in return for repairing some less damaged frames. Given the initiative, old frames begin to appear, but not all are suitable. Avoid large neo-rococo or swept frames at first, or indeed mouldings that are not pleasing to the eye. Most will be 19th-century frames, some of which were superb, particularly those which, under the influence of Ruskin, echo Renaissance designs or classical (i.e. early 17th-century) motifs. Gothic frames inspired by Pugin and Viollet le Duc sometimes appear. The more you learn about ornament evolution and fashion the better. Only frames finished in burnished water gilding, as bright and shining as an Inca treasure, should be avoided, for fear of harming the extremely delicate leaf, but these are very rare indeed. In the whole of the Tate Gallery in London I am aware of only one. Otherwise, with old battered oil gilding, or heavily ormolu varnished gilt, no harm is done and, indeed, the frame will lose generations of polluted fallout. Donors can be reassured on this point. As an act of courtesy I usually do odd small repairs and a refreshening of the gilded highlights before returning a borrowed frame, and people seem very happy, as indeed they should be.

Opposite above: The smaller frame is adapted from the design motif of a Japanese sword handle. The larger is cast from the longer side of an Italian baroque frame, two moulds being taken, of the inner and outer mouldings. Here they are used together as in the original, but they can be used separately

Opposite below: The frame on top was cast as usual from the longer side of an existing frame. Art deco frames are rare, since very minimal Bauhaus framing was more common at the time (1930)

The frame beneath is modelled on a Vienna Secession frame and copied from a 1905 catalogue. It is an approximation of a Gustav Klimt frame

I have chosen two frames to illustrate the casting of a copy. The first is early Victorian (*c.* 1840) which is straightforward, and the Crystacal cast will form its own rebate, (page 45) since it is wider than a 1 × 1-inch (25 × 25-mm) piece of wood, as can be seen on page 44. The second is an extreme example of French Second Empire exuberance with self-contained corner ornaments (page 44 lower and page 52). The silicone moulds are made similarly but in the second example the card 'shoulders' to hold the edges of the silicone rubber need to extend around the corners of the frame. The finished cast is glued to a flat-topped plain wood moulding, readymade or made from an inverted L of two flat strips glued together. To make the frame longer or shorter, C scrolls have to be cut out and removed or the cast cut and extra scrolls added. This can be seen on page 45. The joins can be fudged with Polyfilla, epoxy putty or gesso pasta.

When dry and trimmed all casts of whatever shape are glued on to suitable strips of timber with a contact adhesive, such as is used for sticking sheets of plastic onto wooden surfaces. Disobey instructions,

A frame, *c.* 1835, prepared for casting one side, with the stiff card 'shoulders' in place: the mould has a running pattern and the four pieces are assembled and joined conventionally

French neo-baroque frame *c.* 1870, with the 'shoulders' extended to include corner ornaments. This is not a running pattern which repeats indefinitely, so the entire wooden structure of the frame must be fully assembled first, and the ornament stuck on in a logical sequence

however, and join the cast and wood when the cement is still wet, not dry, as is usual. By choosing timber narrower than the cast, a strong reliable rebate results, though this is not always suitable and a wooden rebate must be glued to the wood. The casts must be cemented straight, hence joining to the wood when wet. A wide variety of mouldings can be accommodated to wooden strips of 1 × 1 inch (25 × 25 mm) or 2 × 1 inch (50 × 25 mm) with or without added wooden rebate.

When cementing the cast to the wood, lay it on and immediately remove it to see if there is a total glue contact. If not, smear some glue on the blank areas and replace the cast, evenly and carefully.

Illustrations 4 and 8 on page 52 are 2¼ inch (56 mm) wide with added rebates. 5 and 6 need wooden rebates. No. 7 is 1¼ inch (31 mm) and makes its own rebate when cemented to 1 × 1 inch (25 × 25 mm) or 1 × ¾ inch (25 × 19 mm).

On the outside of the frame moulding, measure up from the bottom to the height of the inside 'roof' of the rebate as shown and mark this height at either end with a china graph crayon or a piece of masking tape. A simple variable gauge can be contrived for doing this, a strip of card, measured and cut to the height. Fix a thin strip of wood about 1 inch (25 mm) wide along this implied line, initially with a few hinges of masking tape and then with a couple of small blocks of wood, rubber-cemented onto the outside of the frame beneath the strip of wood and onto the bottom of the strip (see illustration). On short pieces of moulding on small frames, up to about 2 feet (610 mm) long, lumps of warm plasticene are sometimes adequate. The repared frame needs to remain as it is for up to two days, depending on how soon the second or third coat of silicone rubber is applied.

There will be a hair crack where the two shoulder strips join the frame, under the rebate and along the outside. These must be sealed since the silicone rubber is extremely ductile and will flow wherever it can. The simplest way to seal this is to prepare a watery mixture of dental plaster in an egg-cup, stir and allow it to thicken to a thin cream. Paint this into the crack with a water-colour brush and wash the brush thoroughly at once. When the plaster stiffens a little, but before it has set, wipe off the surplus with the tip of a finger. Do not disturb the wooden shoulder strips.

Silicone rubber is a synthetic substance consisting of a heavy white cream, like a thick oil paint. To this is added a small quantity of hardener which causes it to set, a process that takes four or five hours in a warm room. Being full of silicones, no oil or petroleum jelly is needed for rigid coats, but a soft rubber is safer than a hard one. Silicone rubber is prepared in different consistencies and I have found that RTV 700, manufactured by the General Electric Company, Waterford, New York, USA, is most satisfactory. It is sold in London by Alec Tiranti, the sculptors' suppliers, of 21 Goodge Place, London. Of the two hardening agents available, the green is the more ductile.

The instructions on the packaging for mixing silicone rubber and hardener are impossibly inconvenient for small amounts at a time. Even the most meticulous craftsman would baulk at them. A quarter of a tsp (1·25 ml) of hardener to two tbs (30 ml) of the thick white liquid silicone rubber is enough. This should serve generously for the first coat to a mould 2 inches (50 mm) wide and 3 feet (900 mm) long, or a bit more depending on its design. Mix very thoroughly until the rubber is an even pale green colour, using a small cheap hog brush, and paint it onto the pattern and the two thin wooden shoulders,

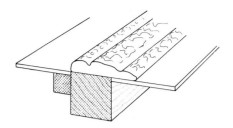

How to fix 'shoulders' for rubber casting so as to cast only the top layer of ornament. This also illustrates how an overhanging Crystacal cast can form a strong rebate on a wooden base

Tamping in the length of bandage into the silicone rubber

Finished silicone mould in a tray made of wooden strips to hold it firmly without distortion

Preparing a more complex plaster tray to support a deeper silicone rubber mould more snugly

already lightly but totally greased, and leave for 6 to 10 hours to set, in a warm room. In the cold it takes longer. A second coat or a thickening on the highlights can be given when the rubber has firmly gelled but is still a bit sticky.

If there are rich highlights, i.e. particularly high ridges or tops of the pattern, prepare about a quarter the original amount of rubber and paint only on the highlights, since the fluid silicones flow into hollows, leaving the highlights with a very thin coat. If you have mixed too much, don't waste it, brush it all on.

When the last brushing of the mixture is set or even half-set, prepare for the final coat by setting by you a 1-inch (25-mm) and a 2-inch (50-mm) roll of ordinary openweave bandage, and a pair of small sharp scissors. Cut off some 6-inch (150-mm) lengths of 1-inch (25-mm) bandage, enough to stretch about one-and-a-half times along either side of the prepared moulding. Prepare a further mix of silicone rubber, slightly more than the first, and paint it on. Take one of the lengths of 1-inch (25-mm) bandage and lay it along the shoulder, so that its edge rises up about $\frac{1}{4}$ inch (6 mm) onto the edge of the moulding, as shown. If too little extends onto the frame it will not lie flat, but will tend to stand up in a ridge. This depends on the shape of the moulding. In that case, sacrifice some of the shoulder area of bandage and move it further onto the moulding. The shoulder areas can easily be extended before completion.

Tap the bandage down with the brush, forcing the coat of rubber through the mesh. Take the next strip of bandage and overlap it by an inch (25 mm) or so and continue until the whole of both sides is bandaged, extending $\frac{3}{4}$ inch (19 mm) from either end. Tamp each successive strip of bandage down with a lightly loaded brush, do not stroke it or it will lift. Cover the top with overlapping 4-inch (100-mm) to 6-inch (150-mm) strips of 2-inch (50-mm) bandage but wherever the bandage has to surmount a highlight or spread down into a large hollow, make a small cut, halfway across it with the scissors, as shown. This is to prevent a pleat which would hold an air bubble and weaken the mould. Some skill and judgment is needed to determine where to snip, but generally anywhere the bandage is not likely to lie flat in order to bond onto the earlier layer of silicone rubber.

Sometimes one top layer of wider bandage is enough. More often two layers are needed. In any case all the snip cuts must be covered with small squares of bandage. Always give a second layer of bandage to the sides of the moulding, extending onto either shoulder. It is an enormous advantage to have access to the mould when it is half or three-quarters set. At this stage it becomes sticky and the bandage can be pressed down, possibly expelling squeaking little bubbles of air, to form a compressed skin. When completely dry, which can take up to 12 hours in cold weather, it can be peeled off gently, examined and replaced until a bed can be made for it. The brush should be wiped as dry as possible and cleaned in acetone. This is not a complete solvent, but at least it allows the brush a longer life.

If the mould is fairly flat in cross-section, take a piece of timber half an inch (12 mm) wider and glue two strips of $\frac{1}{4} \times \frac{1}{4}$-inch (6 × 6-mm) timber a fraction wider than the mould on each side so that the mould can lie gently supported on the sides and bottom (see illustrations).

If a $\frac{1}{4} \times \frac{1}{4}$-inch (6 × 6-mm) strip of timber is too deep for the mould, use a shallower narrow strip of hardboard or plane the $\frac{1}{4} \times \frac{1}{4}$-inch (6 × 6 mm) to the right depth so that the mould can rest in it, gently supported under the shoulders, with its outside base gently touching the base length of the timber, as shown.

If the moulding has an undulating side profile, a more subtle supporting bed is needed, made from plaster on a wooden base. When the silicone rubber mould is finished, remove it and then replace it on the moulding. Mix some plaster of Paris (dental plaster is fine-grained and quick-setting) and, waiting until it has begun to thicken, rapidly spread on a layer ¼ inch (6 mm) deeper than the highest point. Work fast, using a suitable flat knife.

If the plaster hardens too much, stop and make a fresh mix. A few cupfuls will usually do the whole job. When this is set, mix a little more and spread it over the first layer of plaster and while it is still creamy wet, lay a strip of glass on it, moving it slightly from side to side to settle it down. When this is set hard (about 20 minutes) lift the glass; the plaster and rubber will lift off together (see illustration). The rubber can be peeled out of the plaster bed, which will come away from the glass if left for half an hour. The process can be speeded by putting the plaster and glass under a tap for a few seconds, when the plaster will slide off, sometimes too quickly. When the plaster bed is set but still wet, it can be trimmed along the edges with a rasp, a surform plane or a sharp knife. Be careful, since it is weak and heavy at this stage, although a simple break or two does not matter.

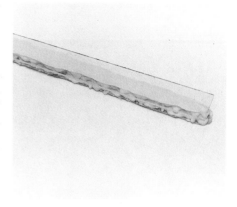

Laying a glass strip along the wet plaster 'tray' to lend a smooth surface for cementing the plaster form onto a strip of wood

It must be left to dry in a warm room, after which it can be stuck to a piece of wood for strength. Use a contact adhesive for speed and convenience, but not as directed on the package. Cover the wood or the smooth side of the plaster fairly generously, whichever is the lesser in area and press together; because it is still liquid the position can be adjusted precisely (see illustration). If the plaster has warped in drying, press it down heavily with both hands, causing it to crack with a hair-line and lie flat. The crack is harmless. With the wooden bed or the plaster wood bed, paint the edges with petroleum jelly, adequately but not to excess. Lay back the rubber mould and it is ready to store or use. If the length of moulding taken from the old frame is too short, two casts must be carefully taken, stuck down on a wider strip of hardboard, smooth side up, and joined together carefully as the pattern dictates and stuck down with contact adhesive. The joint must be fudged with modelling clay or polyfilla, and modelled or carved into reasonable continuity. Even relative beginners seem to manage this quite well.

The completed plaster tray on a wood base, showing the form of the outside of the silicone rubber mould

In casting a positive from a reverse mould, with a few exceptions if the reverse mould is rigid, the casting material must be flexible. It must bend to get it out; or the mould can be flexible, so as to be peeled off a rigid cast. The former is the old technique, which must still be used in certain circumstances which will be explained later. For the second a plasterlike substance can be poured liquid and allowed to set hard. It must be very hard, to resist scratching or scuffling: much harder than plaster of Paris and finer than the various plasters used by builders. Alex Tiranti, the main suppliers in London of sculptors' materials, sell just such under the name of Crystacal. British Gypsum describe it as alpha produced hemi hydrate gypsum plaster. Herculite is a similar substance.

Get a few strips of ordinary window glass cut, 2½ inches wide by about 3 feet long (60 mm × 1 metre), and keep one by you. Prepare a flexible plastic cup by sawing off the top of a washing detergent container, leaving a beaker about 6–7 inches (150–180 mm) high. Fill this two-thirds full with cold water and gently shake in some measures of Crystacal with the help of a small tin can (tomato purée cans are useful for this) until the water nearly reaches the top. Leave it to stand until the air bubbles stop and carefully pour off the milky water until a white sludge remains (looking like a wet meringue). Pour the watery top into a plastic bucket and *never* down a plughole, since this thin whey will wreck any plumbing system. After a day, clear water can be poured off and the residue knocked out into a refuse bin. The sludge in the beaker should be stirred thoroughly with a cheap brush and is now properly proportioned for use. This is the most reliable mixing method, easy, foolproof and automatically ensures its own correct proportions.

Paint the inside of the silicone rubber mould generously with the white sludge. No greasing is necessary but the non-stick silicones tend to reject water and the brush minimizes tiny bubbles and small hollows that might not fill with direct pouring. Now take the beaker in one hand and, using the same brush, paddle out a flow of white sludge along the mould (see illustration). Stop when three-quarters full and, raising the mould and its bed about an inch (25 mm), tap it on the table a few times, shaking out some more tiny bubbles. If insufficient Crystacal has been mixed, make some more, but without delay and pour until the mould is filled nearly to the top. Place the strip of glass on top of it and push it backwards and forwards a couple of times until the shape of the mould opening shows through the glass. This ensures a constant thickness in successive castings. Some of the Crystacal will squeeze out and form stalactites down the side of the bed. Run a finger along this, under the shelving glass, to remove most of it. These accretions can seal the cast to the bed of the mould and if allowed to harden will make the removal of the cast more hazardous. If the silicone mould has been taken directly from a frame, it will be open at either end. These openings must be stopped with a knob of modelling clay or plasticene. If it is a secondary cast, i.e. two short lengths joined together as mentioned earlier, or perhaps widened by the addition of a narrow wooden fillet or any such, the rubber and bandage can go around the ends, blocking them effectively.

Setting time is about 40 minutes and cannot be hurried. Turn the mould and its bed glass downwards. Remove the bed, cracking off any stalactites that remain, peel off the silicone mould carefully and replace it in its bed. If left for about half an hour the cast will come away from the glass, but it can be freed quickly by swamping it with loaded brushes of water. It must be well dry before its next use.

It sometimes happens that a centre band of ornament must be abstracted from the centre of a wide 19th-century frame. Such a strip, 2 inches (51 mm) wide or more, can be used on its own or fixed to a new wooden matrix of wooden strips and mouldings to taste, as in the original or otherwise. A strip of ornament is something to be used at will. It will be impossible to fit shoulder strips down the centre of a frame, so ignore them and take a straight silicone cast, keeping the back as even as possible, brush the area thinly with petroleum jelly first. It will have no edge to give depth to the positive cast, so trim the edges and lay a thin strip of wood of the desired thickness against either edge and glue them down lightly to a smooth board or glass with the silicone reverse mould snugly in the middle as illustrated. Grease the wooden strips, fill the deepened mould, remove the glass

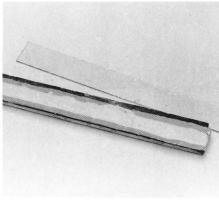

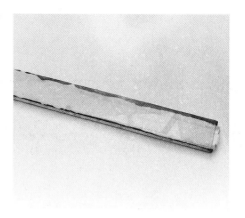

The first step is to paint, and then puddle the Crystacal into the mould

The mould is slightly over-filled. Tap it in order to remove any bubbles

Lay the glass on top and move back and forward to expel any surplus

After setting turn the mould upside down

Remove the cast and the flexible mould from the tray

Gently peel off the mould

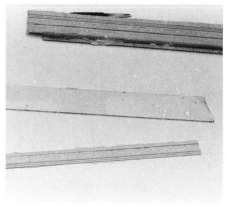

The cast remains on the glass, held there by suction

Clean the edges roughly. The cast will come away when dryer or douche with water for speed

When half-dry the cast can be trimmed with a Surform tool or rasp when set, prise off the wooden strips and take the cast off the rubber. It will now have a chosen constant thickness. Trim the edges smooth and cast again in silicone rubber. If it seems necessary, tape off the areas of the frame before beginning the process.

Mouldings can be designed or copied from exhibitions unavailable for casting, particularly 'running patterns' (repeated designs). Capacity depends on modelling ability, but useful designs can be copied from drawings or gallery photographs. Part of a Spanish baroque frame is illustrated here, made up from a photograph of old Madrid framers' drawings. This most gracious of frames, dark with sombre soft gold in places, is most flattering to portraits or even rich and more formal abstracts. The second example is a flat, mid-19th-century Gothic frame adapted from one in the Scottish National Gallery, Edinburgh. Both were reconstructed similarly, with modelling clay on a flat board. The centre and corner ornaments of the Spanish frame were straightforward, the rubber mould being taken directly from the greased clay. The outer and inner border, characteristic of this type of frame, consist of repeated units. One of each was modelled and cast in silicone rubber. From time to time, over nearly a week, a cast was taken from each mould in quick-setting dental plaster. These were sandpapered clean and struck down at short intervals on a strip of wood, against a straight-edge. The two lines of motifs were then cast in silicone rubber.

The Gothic frame, shown here in rather extreme use, was reconstructed from the main features of a frame on display. Since it exactly suited a series of small dark mid-19th-century landscapes brought by students, I decided that a copy would be useful in a variety of ways. The flat frame was quattrocento in style, a flat with an inner and outer moulding with a running pattern of gilt Gothic 'stonework'. One unit of this double ogee tracery was drawn, carefully centred so that it could be accurately joined to cast duplicates and cut out in mounting board. The clay was modelled on this and cast in silicone rubber. Casts were taken from this in quick-setting dental plaster and joined together, glued to a board and tidied up. A silicone mould was then taken of the assembly and set in a bed as described earlier. Frail to handle when cast, it became strong when glued to the wooden flat of the moulding.

Both these designs are soft in contour and easy to model. More detailed units of pattern should first be modelled and cast in plaster. Make a little clay wall around the unit and pour in dental plaster in a thin creamy state, always adding plaster to water and pouring off the surplus 'whey'. Tap to remove air bubbles. The reverse shape can then be crisped with small tools, sharpened small screwdrivers, chisels made by hammering the end of nails, filing and sharpening. Squeezes can then be taken from the oiled mould with clay, and mounted on a board and reproduced as earlier. If the pull is difficult to extract (its back must be smooth), fill the mould with an epoxy putty and chip away the mould when the cast has hardened, not forgetting to grease it first. A variety of Renaissance patterns, undulates, grecos and so on, can be produced in this way. Irregular shapes can be reversed by first modelling and casting and then making a paper template of the cast and turning it upside down to get the exact outline for the reverse.

Any intelligent framer can extend this technology as needs demand given a reasonable knowledge of art history or reference books.

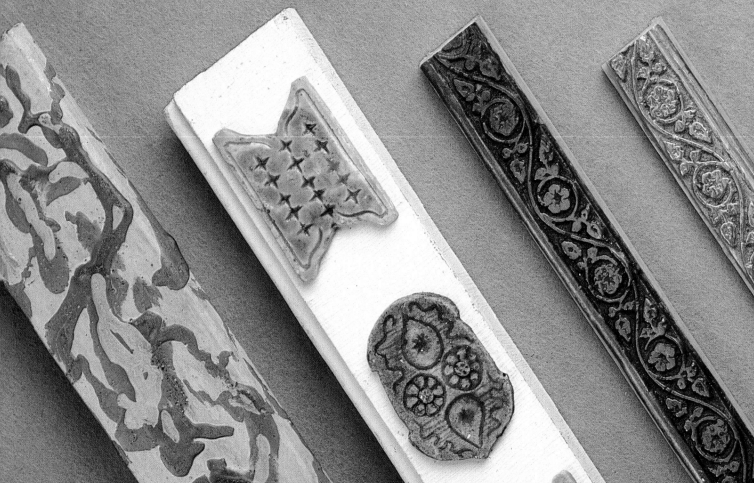

Far left: A frame from the neo-baroque second empire

Left: Chinese corner ornaments, adapted from a Museum exhibit

Below, from left to right: Variegated colours in gesso; Persian tile pattern; undulating renaissance bronze; undulating renaissance in gilt; Chinese moulding in green jade glaze; imitation tortoise shell; Chinese cartouch

Museums are a prime source. The Chinese frame (see illustration) was taken from a bronze Ming ritual vessel (1368–1643), a unit of the repeating design being copied in a sketchbook. This unit was modelled in clay, although wax can also be used. Crisp detail was avoided in the clay and the piece resembled a tile in low relief 1×6 inches (25×150 mm). A silicone mould was made of this and half-a-dozen plaster casts taken. These were carefully stuck to a strip of glass and the pattern smoothed and sharpened by carving. The joints were patched with soft plaster and the background cross-hatched with an awl and a sliding setsquare, a technique used on gesso on neo-rococo 19th-century frames.

Many basic designs are common to a wide range of cultures: a Greek key pattern can be found in Korean and Japanese design and I have seen and used a Papuan bark cloth design which is pure Jugenstil-Klimt. The finished pattern was then cast in silicone rubber and the resulting frames were finished in a lustrous green transparent glaze to resemble jade or a celadon pottery glaze. Much later I discovered some similar Chinese frames in the Lever Museum, Port Sunlight.

When taking a silicone rubber mould from a corner or centre ornament on a baroque or rococo frame, two successive moulds should be made if the intention is for permanent use rather than a passing repair. If a clay squeeze is taken from the first mould it can be flattened onto a sheet of glass and trimmed, tidied and sharpened, particularly when the clay has dried 'cheese' hard. Lightly oil the mould before taking the squeeze and hold the clay briefly under a cold tap after 'squeezing' it, to wash off some of the oil. Corner and centre ornaments cannot usually be cast in Crystacal, which is rigid. The cast must be flexible when wet to accommodate itself to the slope and curve of a particular frame, and must be pressed or squeezed from the silicone rubber mould in a dough-like gesso composition or paste, which will be described in the section dealing with the repair of old frames, or making parts of certain ornamented ones.

Driven by necessity I had to devise a means for casting designs onto wood in cold poured metals. These are used widely in sculpture and examples are to be seen in most mixed exhibitions, though not usually recognised as such. Cold poured metal sculpture is made of a heavy veneer of metal over fibre glass and polyester resin which polishes, burnishes or can be patinated like a hot poured casting, though the process is much cheaper and can be done by the artist without sending the work to a foundry. The most common metals, in the form of very fine powders, are bronze, brass, nickel, aluminium and copper. A mixture of aluminium and nickel with a touch of brass gives a reasonable silver. The finished objects can be left to gather their own natural discolouration, but for framing, the use of a metal polish every six months or so seems to look better, unless the frame is built in vast proportions.

Adapted to cast mouldings for frames or even furniture, the appearance is unusual, but sufficiently conventional, metal being what it is, as to be reassuringly acceptable. The most outstanding metal frame known to me is a broad flat frame in copper, designed by Holman Hunt for his 'May Morning on Magdalen Tower' in the Lever Gallery, Port Sunlight. Its symbols of Spring, fish, clouds and frogs in low relief strangely do not intrude on the painting, proving that you can break every alleged rule in the book if you know how.

Cold metal castings can be taken from almost any silicone mould of a section of frame moulding already described and bonded on strips of wood. These adapt to a frame moulding in a variety of proportions.

There are specialized books on cold casting in sculpture but, briefly, a suitable amount of polyester resin is activated with its hardener in a small PVC cup (sawn-off detergent container), enough to cover the area in a generous coat. Three or four drops of hardener should be enough. Mix thoroughly and trickle in enough of the special fine metal powder to achieve a thin paste. This is painted onto the mould and allowed to harden (one hour in a warm room, less in hot sunshine). Now mix enough resin and hardener to generously fill the mould nearly level, and add any of the inert filler powders supplied, slate, barytes, chalk, to make a liquid dough, and fill the mould. Carefully set a strip of wood of exactly the same width as the mould on top of the grey goo and press it gently to settle level with the top of the mould. Its edges must be aligned carefully along the edges of the mould. This will take a little longer to set, but the squeezed surplus will indicate when. Peel off the silicone mould and trim the edge surplus with a sharp knife. It will not look very attractive at first until a thin film of resin is scrubbed off with fine steel wool, when the metal will be revealed. The steel wool, however fine, leaves a slightly scored surface and benefits from buffing on a cloth wheel with rouge. Such wheels are available for attachment to electric drills, clamped in a stand, well-known to home handymen. After such a burnishing, it is necessary to clean the surface with the type of metal polish made up into a cotton swab. This removes the rouge embedded in deep undercuts. Do not bother to scour out every little hollow from the beginning of this process. The unpolished hollows add depth by contrast with the metal gleam of the highlights.

It might well be necessary to set a band of metal ornament along the centre of a moulding, necessarily a flat section. In such a case cut a strip of mounting board or a very thin strip of wood and bond this to the casting as just described. Either of these can be handled easily and bonded anywhere with a contact adhesive. If mounting board is used, lay the cast between two pieces of board with a weight, since it tends to curl when curing, which goes on for a few days after it has set.

Polyester resin can be used to produce a very convincing ivory. The prepared resin should be whitened by the addition of titanium oxide pigment and a pinch of yellow ochre pigment and used as a first coat like the metal powder mixture. When the cast has set it should be rubbed with steel wool to expose the colour. It can either be waxed and polished or stained with a very thin umber wash in thin size, rubbed almost clean with a damp cloth and then waxed.

Tortoise, or more properly turtle shell, has been used for ornament in furniture and in some Dutch wave pattern frames, popular in the 17th century. For repairs, a convincing effect can be made by treating a piece of glass with wax and resin-parting lacquer. Paint the glass with resin, faintly tinted with dry pigment yellow ochre, broken in patches by a darker tint and perhaps shaded with a little burnt umber pigment. Streak this with some opaque burnt umber mixed in resin with thinner and translucent added. It is essential to copy from a piece of polished shell, a hand mirror, brush or whatever. Finish off with a couple of coats of clear resin and it can be prised off the glass when set. Sometimes the original shell was set over silver leaf to enhance the translucency.

GESSO, FINISHES AND GILDING

GESSO

IF YOU SCRATCH any ornamental frame, simple or ornate, cast or carved, a layer of red clay will show beneath the old gilt and a thicker layer of white below that again. The latter is liquid gesso, *gesso sottile* (It.) or sometimes in English 'pencil white'. Its purpose is to form a manageable foundation to give a desired texture, smooth, polished or deliberately roughened or textured. The Egyptians used something like it and Cennini's formula written in the 1470s is virtually the same as the one that I describe below. Up to the 16th century it was the universal ground for paintings and is still used on wooden panels. It can consist of little more than powdered chalk (whiting) and glue size, but this is liable to cracking and has a gritty texture, and needs a further refinement.

The addition of some 'slaked' or deadened plaster of Paris makes a critical difference in the behaviour of the liquid gesso. It is made in the following manner from dental plaster for ease and quality. Add a tablespoonful (15 ml) of dental plaster to its own bulk in water. Do not stir, but pour off the watery liquid on top, but not into a drain. Stir and pour the thick cream onto a newspaper and time its setting which will take about 20 minutes. Fill a bucket three-quarters full of water and trickle in about two cupfuls of dental plaster. It is now necessary to stir the thin mixture for more than the setting time of the plaster, perhaps half an hour. Vigorous stirring is not needed. Indeed one can read or do nearby chores, stirring with a stick every minute or so, so as to keep the water white. The plaster tends to sink to the bottom and harden, or half harden, and this must be prevented. Then leave it for several hours and pour or syphon off the clear water on top.

If, after this, it is possible to pour the white cream into narrower jars (preserving jars can be used), the process will continue, but it is easier to pour off two inches (50 mm) of water from a jar than $\frac{1}{4}$ inch (6 mm) of water from a bucket. Eventually a thicker white mud will precipitate, which can be used. Seal the jar to prevent its drying completely. This white mud consists of tiny crystalline particles which make a durable aggregate with the coarser particles of chalk, causing the gesso to paint on creamily and resist cracking or flaking, its two besetting sins.

To assemble the ingredients of the liquid gesso, prepare some size as before, with four tsp (20 ml) to the quarter pint (150 ml) of water and melt in hot water. Put (let us say) two tbsp (30 ml) of gilders whiting (chalk) in a bowl, and one dessertspoon (7 ml) of slaked plaster: 1 to 4. Mix and carefully spill in some hot size, stirring each time. Stop when it is a thick cream. If you add too much size, add more whiting and slaked plaster.

'Monna Vanna' by Dante Gabriel Rossetti.
The frame faintly suggests a renaissance
structure because of the ornamented flats
but it is untypical of Rosetti's more
characteristic and original frame designs

The simple basic frame from Chapter 2, textured in gesso and given a burnt umber tempera wash

The side of a frame cast as Chapter 4 and textured in gesso. The highlights are gilded over dark brown

A gesso textured mount on a 'tray' frame with a transparent wash of colour

Mix thoroughly with a round hog brush and put through a sieve into a tin can. I use curry and spice tins which have a sealable plastic top for easy storing in a fridge. When it sets, it can be liquefied again by standing it in hot water.

To impart a gesso finish to the basic frame described in an earlier chapter, give it a coat of the size used above and allow to dry for half an hour. Then give it a rich coat of gesso and allow that to dry for about an hour in a warm room. Using a plastic nail brush or a plastic throwaway toothbrush, coat one side of the frame, face and side. Allow it to gel for a few moments and brush deeply and methodically, across the face and down the side, leaving dozens of parallel grooves with every stroke. If the gesso has dried too much to register, paint more gesso on the dried area and continue. Do all four sides of the frame and allow to dry thoroughly, that is, when the surface is totally white. Darker patches denote damp spots. Lightly sandpaper stray extruding nodules of gesso, but no more. By doing this the texture will not be removed.

Many different patterns of texture can be effected by experiment; overlapping half circles are attractive. The wider the face the more scope for variations.

In the case of a frame where the mouldings have been cast in Crystacal glued onto wood, size all over face and sides and allow to dry. Do not allow puddles of size to collect in the hollows. When dry, coat only the wood on the sides or on the rebate strip if one is used, with liquid gesso and allow to dry. Gesso would fill up any fine detail in the casting, which will probably be cast from an antique moulding already gessoed. In any case, the Crystacal is sufficiently like the gesso in texture to make little difference. A little on the mitre joints, rubbed down, or on the highlights is permissable.

If a smooth finish is needed on the wooden parts, each coat of gesso (up to three or four) should be rubbed down with a sandpaper block. It needs to be said that in 98 per cent of cases this is neither necessary nor desirable. Certain mouldings demand a smoothness in places, but in most cases a combed texture, such as the one described above, is much more effective either with a colour wash, a glaze or with gold or silver. An agreeable and uncommon effect can be achieved by first covering a flattish minimal frame in gesso and then, when the gesso is still wet, splattering it with some more gesso previously tinted with dry pigment or any water-based paint like gouache or poster colour. Violent extremes of such splattered colour should be avoided on paintings, but for mirrors or exotics striking effects can be achieved in this way.

The top coat of gesso can be tinted with dry pigment or poster colour to an agreeable base colour, giving a deeper 'fresco' quality than an overlaid paint. Dry pigments are sold in colour shops for theatrical scene painting, but artists' suppliers also sell dry pigments. These should be rendered with thin size.

Colour washes

To revert to the simple frame of one-by-one (25 × 25 mm) plus ¼-inch (6-mm) rebate or two-by-one (50 × 25 mm) plus rebate described in Chapter 2, we must now assume that it has been sized and treated with two coats of gesso, one textured. The simplest and one of the most attractive ways to complete it is to give it a transparent colour wash, as if for a water-colour, over the textured white gesso. Choose the colours carefully. As far as possible they should be colours that do not contain white, as with a water-colour painting. If a blue is needed, do not use pure ultramarine, but add a touch of black, even at times a touch of green, for yellow, use yellow ochre. Take some warm size (4 tbs to the quarter pint, 60 ml size to 150 ml water), pour some off and thin with as much hot water. Pour as much as might be needed and a little more into a small, warm vessel and add a fraction of dry colour pigment with the tip of a brush, and stir. Test on a sheet of newspaper for density. The print should read clearly when dry. Transparency is the key.

Modify with other colours to taste, always testing on newsprint, or better, on a spare piece of gessoed wood. Allow for a drop in tone when dry. With a loaded round hog brush, paint on rapidly, not lingering on any area, lest the wettened gesso should soften and mix to a muddy blur and leave to dry face up. The colour will collect deeply in the crevices, and only lightly tint the ridges if at all. When thoroughly dry, wax polish the tinted surface, there is a section about this at the end of this chapter. The textured pattern will stand out, giving the required tone and colour but broken by hundreds of lighter ridges with a pointillist effect. Dry pigment as used for theatrical scene painting is cheapest, but for limited use size tinted from a jar of poster colour may be more convenient.

Glazes

An unusual and attractive finish to certain frames consists of a transparent coloured glaze over a broken or uneven white surface. The surface must be white to give the maximum luminescence to the glaze. It is not an effect to overuse, since it suggests glazed pottery, Chinese porcelain or even jade, but surprisingly it is a satisfactory answer to certain picture problems, mirror glasses and interior decoration.

It consists of suspending, or mixing, a small amount of dry pigment in polyester resin and flooding it onto the surface. The surface being white, the highlights remain lighter and the hollows darker because of the greater depth of the glaze which lies there. A certain control is possible because not all colours are equally effective, those containing white or which are opaque by nature lack sparkle but greens, blues, reds, browns, ochres and even blacks make good glazes.

Prepare half-a-dozen or so pieces of moulding ornament cast in Crystacal, or textured in white gesso. Take a detergent container cut off to form a cup about 3 inches (75 mm) high and half fill it with polyester resin activated by four drops of hardener well stirred. According to the number of colours you wish to experiment with, set out some small dishes. The foil or waxed paper containers used for baking tea cakes or individual tarts are useful. Avoid any plastic other than PVC. Pour a few spoonfuls of the activated resin into each dish, and add a few crumbs of pigment to the first. Let us suppose it is ultramarine blue. Dip a medium hog brush in the dry pigment and stir it in, then test the depth of colour on a piece of paper. It should be pale but definitely blue. Stir in well and test it on a piece of the cast moulding.

Wipe the brush with a rag, clean it in acetone, wipe again and mix some viridian green similarly. Test this out and also perhaps ochre, burnt umber and black, testing each on paper. The result should always be transparent, not solid colour. Coat another piece of casting

Above, clockwise from top left: Northern Renaissance 'Tudor' frame; Neo Rococo with transparent black glaze; Indian painting ornamental ogee frame with grey blue and silver highlights; mid-19th-century gothic frame; gilt on Indian Red; the first and last are from sketches and the remainder are cast from originals

Right: Coloured glazes in polyester resin

Left: Mottling, stippling and sponging on gesso (George Brandreth)

in blue and dab it unevenly with green and let it set. Reverse the process, coating with green and dabbing with blue. Cleaning the brush each time, test out yellow ochre, black and burnt umber unevenly over yellow ochre. Try out a few touches of blue over black. Always wipe and clean your brush immediately or you will soon have a whalebone brush, totally unusable.

These glazes are not paints, they do not dry hard, they set hard. Always use a loaded brush and try tilting the cast to engineer dribbles over which some sort of control is possible. After a few hours in a warm room, examine the results and decide where colours were too dense or the reverse. Indeed there is no right answer, apart from undesirable opaqueness due to too much colour or too violent a colour, which happens most easily using ultramarine blue or red ochre. Keep these tests, together with a pale turquoise made by mixing blue and green, thinned with clear resin if necessary. You will quickly learn how different colours behave in glaze form, but remember that white or anything opaque cannot be used, any more than in aquarelle painting. The cheapest dry pigment is the kind used for theatrical scene painting, where it is tempered with glue size, but many art shops sell tins of pigment with a reasonable range.

When using a glaze on a cast frame, the bare wood should first be sized and given two coats of gesso. The glaze makes a more interesting pattern with greater light diffusion if the top coat of gesso is textured as described earlier.

In general, for light-coloured frames, gesso, tinted or its own normal off-white, is a better final finish than an oil paint, glossy or matt, although two coats of suitably tinted matt emulsion paint are more useful if the frame is being handled a lot, as in a travelling exhibition, since emulsion can be damp-wiped with a detergent. A light coat of gesso can be laid over a darker coat and rubbed away in places with fine steel wool, and then wax polished. This pleasing effect can be reversed. An ornamented frame gessoed grey or any drab tone can be delightfully enlivened by touching the highlights with silver or gold, giving richness with tonal austerity for various kinds of paintings, from Impressionism to Abstract Expressionism.

Opaque glazes and scumbles

A category of finishes, opaque glazes and scumbles, can be carried out with shellac spirit varnishes, but this is such an exhaustive subject, largely related to antique restoration and interior decoration, that an advanced student is recommended to read a specialized book on the subject.

Most of the finishes that are described here, including cold poured metals, equally apply to furniture restoration, brass mouldings, gilding, gesso, *papier maché* trays, Regency fittings, sphinxes, knobs, and so on, even tortoiseshell panels. In restoration, precise categories are blurred, and commonsense takes over.

GILDING

Gilding is one of the most difficult problems for students of framing. It too is considered a specialized matter; I have a lengthy book on the subject by an old and honoured Spanish framemaker and gilder which, he confesses, is incomplete.

It must be emphasized that there is no such thing as a gold or silver paint: only radiator paints. They all darken quickly and have a grainy texture unlike any gilding. Do not use them, whatever the packaging may boast.

Briefly, there are five methods of gilding:
1. Burnishing bronze and size
2. Wax burnishing bronze amalgam
3. Gilding on oil with Schlagg leaf (Dutch metal)
4. Burnished gilding with loose leaf and matt gilding
5. Gilding on oil with loose gold leaf.

Of these, 1 and more particularly 2 are likely to be more useful to most framers, given the present high cost of gold leaf and the slowness of the process, so I will deal with gold leaf last.

Burnishing bronze and size

Burnishing bronze is a golden powder available from gilding suppliers, colour merchants and signwriters' suppliers in different tints, pale to reddish. These tints can be mixed to the desired hue, to suit taste or to match old gilding on repaired frames, a most useful practice of antique picture dealers. Ordinary bronze powders can be used, though they will not produce the same depth of lustre when burnished. Some degree of burnishing is possible however.

All gilding, gold leaf, Schlagg, burnishing bronze or wax amalgam, is translucent, and the colour that lies beneath it is an important part of the hue and tone. It is usually a rusty red colour and can be seen if the gold is rubbed off an old gilt frame. In effect it is a tempera paint of fine-coloured clay rendered with very thin parchment size or sometimes rabbit size. The clay, commonly known as Armenian bole, a mediaeval term, is usually red but can be pink or even black. It is essential for burnished gold leaf but any fine gouache or poster colour rendered with size will do for schlagg leaf, burnishing bronze or wax amalgam. To gild with burnishing bronze, coat the finely steelwooled gesso with a tempera of red ochre poster or gouache, thinned down with size of 2 tsp to the $\frac{1}{4}$ pint. Size and rub with a chamois leather when dry.

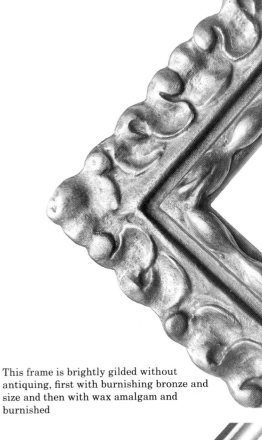

This frame is brightly gilded without antiquing, first with burnishing bronze and size and then with wax amalgam and burnished

Take a little of the thin size in a small warm vessel and add a few drops of methyl alcohol. Spoon in some burnishing bronze, and mix quickly. Most will float on top of the liquid. Flood it over the frame as rapidly as possible with a mop brush and allow to dry, after which it can be burnished with an agate tool.

The act of flooding the surface is important. Much of the powder floats on the liquid which on evaporation deposits it on the surface, as with burnished gold leaf, thus permitting burnishing.

This is mostly suitable for fairly flat unadorned mouldings and takes a little practice to succeed. If, however, a heavily ornamented frame is to be wax-gilded without any antiqueing (i.e. totally gold) a coat of a suitably coloured bronze powder, prepared as above, penetrates into crannies and is a useful undercoat.

Wax burnishing bronze amalgam

Nearest in effect to burnished gold is the wax amalgam. A proprietary version called Treasure Gold (Connoisseur Studio, London, W.11) is stocked by many art shops in small jars in different tones of brightness or redness. Anything in a bottle or tube is to be avoided. Treasure Gold may well suffice for beginners or for anyone with a limited programme since its quality is satisfactory, but for extensive use, a similar preparation can be made at home much more cheaply.

This badly damaged and repaired frame was similarly gilded with burnishing bronze mixed in size and then with wax amalgam. It was then polished with lambswool and burnished with an agate tool

Flake some unbleached beeswax the volume of a walnut into a clean can and add about a quarter of that volume of carnauba wax, flaked off with a penknife into a customary brittle powder. Slightly more than cover the wax mixture with white spirit (naphtha or mineral spirit or turps substitute). Place on a gentle hotplate or very low gas ring covered with wire mesh and melt to complete dissolution, which takes a few minutes. Have a square of warmed glass ready, and make a pyramid of burnishing bronze with a dent in the top, having mixed two different tones of gold to taste if necessary. This can be modified later. The can of wax will be hot, so hold it with pliers and pour some wax into the crater. Work this with a palette knife or a flexible kitchen knife until a smooth thick paste results, adding more wax or powder to achieve this end. Do not spare the palette knifing to get a homogeneous mass. Smear a fingertipful on black newsprint headlines and if these are obliterated scoop the mass into a small airsealed jar.

Airsealing is important to avoid evaporation. Seal the jar in a small freezer bag for extra safety, and it will keep indefinitely. If it dries too hard for easy application, scrape it onto a warm piece of glass and work in a few drops of white spirit with a knife and reseal. To make a useful silver amalgam, use aluminium powder with a little pale-gold bronze powder added, to taste. Silver is warmer in tone than most people realize. In mixing the paste the point to stop adding powder is reached just before it becomes friable or crumbly. The aim is to get in as much metal as possible without drying the paste. If the paste does become too friable, then add a fraction more wax and work in until satisfied.

To apply the amalgam, use the pad of the forefinger which is warm and subtle. Do not lift a lump or gobbet, just a thick coating on the finger pad. Work this onto all the prepared surface as firmly as possible, concentrating at first on the highlights. The finger is best, but for odd corners, hollows and ridges, a cheap small hog or similar brush, cut down to $\frac{1}{4}$ inch (6 mm) can be used. After about an hour in a warm room, the white spirit will evaporate. The longer it is left the better; then it can be vigorously polished, preferably with a 3-inch (75-mm) square of woolly sheepskin or a traditional soft yellow cotton duster. After some days the highlights can be burnished with an agate tool.

Antiqueing

Many, if not most, ornamented frames look better and serve brightly coloured paintings better if they are antiqued. There are various ways of doing this, but with wax gilding the simplest is to use a less reactive colour than red for the bole coat over the gesso: warm brown to burnt umber is a useful colour scale. Use as previously directed and apply the wax amalgam over the highlights only. Apply lightly and evenly with gentle strokes of the finger pad, and avoid a heavy smear which is almost impossible to remove. After several hours, polish as described earlier. The hollows and crevices will remain dark brown, like centuries of smoky accretion. If they are too violent in dark contrast, stipple on a little gold with the previously described cut-down brush, after partly exhausting its charge on a piece of newspaper.

As mentioned earlier, if an entirely gold surface is needed, as for a mirror glass, flood on a coat of burnishing bronze in size after

Opposite: A selection of mouldings dating from the Renaissance to present day, including a Chinese and a Persian example

preparing, and rub down with a piece of chamois and then wax-gold the highlights extensively.

The agate tool mentioned above is usually thought of as a burnisher for gold leaf laid on sized bole. It can however be used on burnishing bronze with size and to excellent effect on wax gold amalgam, a fact not generally known. Its effect on silver amalgam is total, turning the previously lambswooled buffed surface into a sheath of deep lustrous silver. Used on a colour wash over textured gesso it polishes the ridges, darkening their tone where the tool touches and giving the effect of a polished stone, hardwood or a variety of natural substances. The 'agate' can be bought from a gilders' suppliers in several shapes of which the hooked 'claw' has a more general use for ornamented frames, since by selecting the part of the stone best suited to the contour, it is the most versatile. The 'flat' is for flat areas alone and the pencil is for small grooves etc., but the claw does most of the work. In general, using wax amalgam it is the main highlights, cabochons and shallow curved hollows that reflect the light most, and if these glow softly when walking past, they have achieved their purpose. Rub gently and firmly on the raised and gently hollowed areas, taking their shape into account, not haphazardly. The surfaces will darken and become more lustrous, a process that somehow gives great satisfaction. There will be times when the highlights are small in area and the surface is so broken with intricacies that there will be no great advantage in using a burnisher. The lambswool polisher will be enough.

All gold substitutes are liable to tarnish and need some protection from air pollution and finger smears, so does gold leaf, although it endures better. Wax gilded frames in one's possession can be given a rub of new wax amalgam every few years and buffed up which takes a matter of minutes.

Any varnish, even ormolu (Fr. *or moulu*) varnish tends to diminish the quality, but if a very thin size is sprayed on the frame with a plastic flower spray for house plants, it acts as a good protector. A mixture of very thin size and thinned ormolu varnish is somewhat more robust if a great deal of handling is needed. Somehow a light spray alters the surface less than a loaded brush. Frames finished with gold leaf should be treated similarly.

Gilding on oil with Schlagg leaf (Dutch metal)

Schlagg or Dutch metal leaf is a 19th-century substitute for gold leaf, used rather similarly and sold in books 6 inches (150 mm) square, loose and transfer, between sheets of tissue paper. It is a small fraction of the price of gold leaf and might be useful for practice, though it is cruder in use and far less effective in its intention than wax amalgam. Its brassy finish is only acceptable, and here I speak personally, after severe antiqueing or distressing, and it must be sealed outside and inside with shellac or thin cellulose to minimize oxidation.

Finish the frame with gesso well rubbed down and give it two coats of orange shellac and a coat of red ochre or Venetian red acrylic paint, well thinned but opaque, and rub down with 0001 steel wool. For convenience, for a first try-out, give it an even coat of Japan gold size without flooding in the hollows. The given drying time is two hours, but temperature can lessen this by up to a half. Do not coat the entire frame unless it is very small, since it will dry before you finish laying the Dutch metal leaf. When a finger tip placed on the surface can detect no wetness but only a sticking feeling that snaps when the finger is pulled away, it is ready for laying the leaf. Unlike gold leaf, Dutch metal can be handled, though with care. It can be cut or torn to suitable sizes or strips, depending on the ornament or lack of it. A small heap of talc (baby powder) in which to dip the finger tips now and then is very useful. Lay the leaf, overlapping somewhat, tamping it down with a cotton-wool ball wrapped in a piece of gauze.

Clean it with a soft dry hog brush and try to stick down small fragments over 'faults' where the leaf has not taken. If these are dry, dab them with some more Japan size with a small brush while you are coating the next section of frame. The finished effect will be brassy and garish. A coat of orange shellac thinned in methylated spirit to which a tincture of warm brown spirit soluble analine dye has been added will tone it down; or a thin transparent wash of burnt umber in a watery rabbit size with the highlights wiped clean with a warm damp sponge, or a combination of the two. A spattered effect can be achieved by loading a soft brush with some ivory black in thin rabbit size and tapping the brush handle with a small piece of wood over the frame. Practice the splash or dot control first, on some paper or spare moulding. Always finish Dutch metalled frames with two coats of clear or orange shellac to seal them from oxidization.

An effective all over gilt effect can be obtained by giving a coat of slow-setting oil size or quick-setting Japan size over the twice shellacked frame and pouncing its tacky surface with an appropriate bronze gold powder in a screw ball of nylon stocking. The surplus is brushed off onto a newspaper and salvaged.

Silver leaf is not satisfactory because of tarnishing. A silver leaf containing a trace of gold is sometimes available and is safer, but nowadays aluminium leaf, laid on oil, is both cheap and safe. For plain frames a very smooth surface is needed and on an ornamental surface the highlights should be silky smooth. Silver finishes seem to need the glow of regimental silver, otherwise they look drab. Over ornament it is often advantageous to give the frame a diffuse coat of burnt umber in thin size. This gives the effect of oxidized undercuts and hollows if the highlights are wiped clean with a damp sponge and rubbed clear with a soft cotton cloth.

Gilding with gold leaf

Gilding with gold leaf is an expensive, skilled and slow process which produces startling results, too strong for most paintings. A newly gilded frame is as shocking as Tutenkhamon's gold when Carter first shone his torch into the tomb. Since the Renaissance most gilt frames have had their primal brightness reduced with the help of dark-tinted varnishes or tinted size washes, as secular painting made the nature of the subject, originally sacred, less important, and the nature of the painting more so. For a couple of decades in the middle of the 19th century, bright gilding came into fashion as the new industrial middle classes tried to exhibit their recent opulence, the Barbizon frame in France and the heavy spandrelled ovals or tondos. The spread of realism and impressionism quickly killed this taste, and even heavily ornamented frames were toned down so as to complement rather than swamp the painting. The nature and use of mirror glass frames is different. In the 18th century the widespread fashion for glass in bright rococo or neo-classical frames helped to lighten the

The early Victorian frame now assembled and gilded with wax amalgam, leaving the background in burnt umber (Portrait of Kathleen Behan)

Copy in Crystacal of a small period Italian frame on a wooden base. The entire ornament was cast as one

Aluminium leaf is used instead of silver to avoid tarnish. The leaf is laid, using a fold of card for lifting

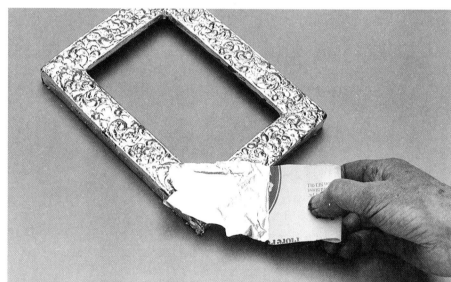

The leaf is damped down with a piece of cotton wool or soft brush. The wooden backing was fully assembled and pinned before cementing to the Crystacal

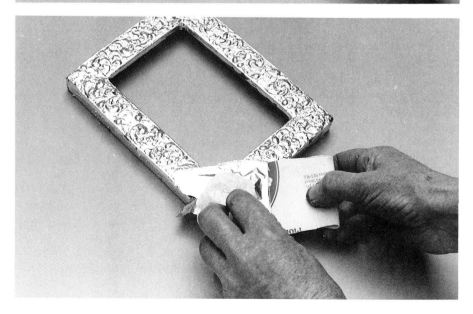

depressing gloom of large salons and galleries lit only by candles. There are three kinds of gilding with gold leaf:

1. *Oil gilding* in which the leaf is bonded by a sticky oil varnish called oil size and applied when the oil size is almost dry, like Dutch metal leaf.
2. *Water gilding* in which the leaf is bonded by depositing it on a layer of water over the clay, which when wet has enough adhesion in itself. Sometimes a very thin animal size is used instead of water.
3. *Matt gilding* which is used on flat insets and consists of two layers of gilt, laid perfectly with thin animal size. It is the most difficult to do, but fortunately less often needed nowadays, even in repair work, so it is not dealt with here.

Oil gilding

Oil gilt cannot be burnished, but water gilding can. Matt gilding is bound by water size in such a way as to keep the finish dull, deep and flawless. Since oil gilding is easier, it was and is common to oil gild an ornamented frame and to pick out chosen highlights in the ornament with burnished gilt so that the frame sparkles in the light as only polished gold can. Gold leaf is immensely thin and cannot be touched when loose. An ounce of gold can be made to cover 240 sq ft: 1/240,000 inch. Ornamented frames need only one layer of leaf. Matt gold on flats requires two layers.

The basic tools and materials are as follows:

1. Book of loose gold leaf. Transfer leaf is unsuitable.
2. Gilder's cushion. This is a small board slightly cushioned and covered in fine suede leather. It includes a draught screen, usually of parchment, with loops to hold a knife and a tip (see below).
3. Gilder's knife for cutting the leaf.
4. Gilder's tip. A flat soft brush with a cardboard handle for lifting the leaf.
5. Agate burnishing tool. These come in different shapes.
6. Brushes. The more the better, but at least a hog mop, a round hog and a gilder's mop.

The expendable materials are:

7. Oil size, Japan gold size.
8. Armenian bole. A red earth sometimes in lumps that must be ground in a mortar or, more commonly, ground wet in a sealed can.
9. A packet of Russian tallow which is used in minute quantities.

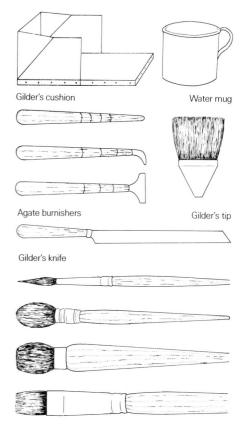

Gilder's cushion

Water mug

Agate burnishers

Gilder's tip

Gilder's knife

Sable, mop and hog brushes

Unlike textured finishes, gold leaf conceals nothing and emphasizes every tiny fault. So whether you are repairing an old frame or finishing a new one, either needs a fine finish. An old frame must be cleaned with acetone and rubbed smooth with steel wool, and gessoed lightly to avoid filling in too much detail. Even a new ornamented frame, cast and assembled as described earlier, should be gessoed carefully, with one good coat of gesso and then a coat on the main highlights only, as well as flats and sides. Cracks should be filled in with a putty made from slightly thinned gesso mixed with some gilder's whiting. Undercuts from slightly risen ornament on old frames should be filled.

A partly repaired Victorian frame with the outer edge painted in yellow ochre mixed with size. This makes it easier for the gilder to handle the work

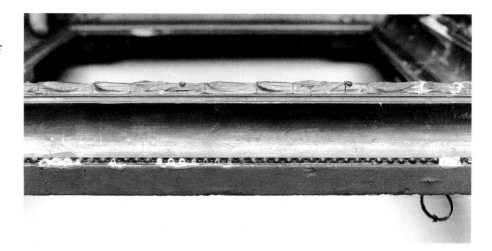

The frame now needs a coat of Armenian bole or gilder's 'clay' which if ground wet is called *assiette d'oré*. If it is in dry lumps it must be powdered with a pestle and mortar to a stiff paste with water and squeezed through a nylon stocking to a red mud like the assiette d'oré, then thinned to a paintable cream with size water. Parchment size is best and can be bought made up in good art shops or gilders' suppliers. Otherwise, genuine parchment clippings are washed and boiled in water for an hour or so until they go into a gel when cool, store this in a fridge.

If parchment size is unobtainable, a thin rabbit size can be used, 3 tsp (15 ml) to the quarter pint (150 ml) and filtered through nylon. Make double the amount in two separate jars if burnishing is desired.

It is common practice to paint the lower part of the outside of gilded ornamented frames in a tempera of yellow ochre with size, acrylic might do. This leaves an area for gripping and diminishes the luminosity of the edges against the wall. Masking tape will give a clean, level line.

Put the prepared size and bole in a small foil dish, floating in a saucer of warm water, and paint it over the frame, avoiding the yellow ochre strips. Carefully smooth it with 0001 steel wool and meticulously brush away the grit, one speck of which could be disastrous for the gold leaf.

Label the size jar and store in a fridge. Warm the second jar and add to it a piece of Russian tallow the size of a pea and amalgamate it, give the frame two coats of this and label and store the size in a fridge.

In order to kill two birds with one stone I am assuming that you are about to oil gild an ornamented frame and put in burnished highlights in water gilding in the mediaeval manner. In the following, use all, or subtract, whatever you choose.

Oil gold size is a boiled oil varnish which tack dries either in 47 hours or 14 hours. That is to say it is ready for about one to two hours' manipulation following those times, depending on which one is found convenient. While teaching, I was forced to use Japan gold size, which tack dries in about two hours, or even less. All these oil mordants respond to temperature and humidity; the higher the temperature, the quicker they respond, which can be either an advantage or a nuisance. For a preliminary experiment, the quick Japan size might be more convenient but, being full of siccatives (drying agents), it darkens quicker, like a bitumen Victorian picture varnish.

If you are using Japan size experimentally, give a first coat and allow to dry, some will sink into porous areas. The second coat should be fit for adhesion when tack dry. If you are using the slower oil size, first give a coat of orange shellac varnish, which is soluble in methylated spirits, and then a coat of the oil size. Japan size can become tack dry in as little as an hour or slightly more, in a warm dry room. The oil size should be estimated by the instructions on the can. Either way, the moment of truth has arrived when all stickiness has gone, but a fingertip on an unimportant piece of the surface makes a snapping sound when pulled away. If using Japan size only, prepare about 6 inches (150 mm) of moulding, any more will dry too much.

Lay on the oil or Japan size very evenly, avoiding puddles in hollows. Squeeze the hog brush and go over the surface to distribute it evenly. Always clean the brushes at once. White spirit for oil or Japan size and methyl alcohol for shellac. Then wash with detergent and hot water and wipe dry. If the highlights are to be burnished, carefully wipe them clean with methyl alcohol on a rag. Gold will not stick on such spots, which are treated separately. Choice of highlights depends on experience and common sense. In general, convex lumps and soft curves on corner or centre ornaments yield the richest results.

To lay the oil gilt, place the leaf book open by the gilder's cushion, near the frame, and slide off a leaf on to the cushion with the knife, blowing gently in its centre to flatten it. With a gentle horizontal action, slice the leaf into two or three strips, not using the knife point. Take the tip and rub it on the top of your head or down your cheek a few times and touch it to one side of the leaf slice. The thin sheet of gold adheres lightly to the tip hairs by virtue of the static electricity generated by rubbing it on the hair or skin.

Where and what size slice depends on the frame pattern, but start with smallish pieces. Start over the outside frame edge, advancing into the frame face. Static electricity in the tip should catch the piece of leaf and hold it until its opposite edge can be gently touched to the frame, when the tip can be gently withdrawn. Always allow the leaf to fall into hollows. Be prepared for tears and tantrums at first and a degree of spoilation, but after a few hours things will improve. Like teaching someone to walk a tightrope, a few do's and don'ts are useful, but the rest is up to nature.

An additional soft brush is useful to coax the leaf down, particularly in hollows. If the brush or the tip edge collect any stickiness they must be wiped with methyl alcohol and dried. When a generous area is covered, tamp it down with a cotton-wool swab and when the tacky area is covered, brush the gold fragments on to a newspaper. Some of these can be used to spot out the many little 'faults' that occur. These always happen, but they will be worse at first. When preparing a further section of frame, or another frame as the case may be, carefully smear these fault patches with dabs of oil or Japan size before patching.

Water gilding
If you are burnishing highlights or soft ridges, these have already been cleaned and must be coated with some bole made from the first size (without tallow) thinned by about one third with hot water. Make sure it is fluid and warm when applying; avoid grit, and rub down with a fragment of chamois leather. Apply a second thin coat of bole mixed

Gilding materials: a gilder's cushion, knife, tip, book of leaf and brushes

Schlagg or Dutch metal leaf is used in this sequence for greater visibility. The leaf is lifted on to the cushion using the knife

The leaf is laid on the cushion ready for cutting

Lifting the leaf with a gilder's tip, a knack soon learnt

Laying the leaf on the prepared moulding taking care to work from the edge

Tamping down the leaf with a soft mop brush, and the faults filled in later. A similar technique is used for water gilding

with a little of the tallowed size and rub down similarly when dry. The size in the bole is enough, or nearly enough, to hold the thin leaf of gold. If the water is hard, boil it and cool it to barely warm. A teaspoonful (5 ml) of the first size dissolved in a cup of this water when still hot is probably the best medium, though some prefer water alone.

Cut the leaf to suit the shapes and flood a small area with a loaded brushful of the water tinctured with size, and drop on the leaf. It will float briefly on the skin of the water and be deposited gently and evenly over the area. Proceed in this way and after a few hours in a warm room the areas can be burnished with the agate to the brightness of a yellow mirror. It should reflect light onto a piece of paper angled beside it. Burnishing should be systematic, backwards and forwards. Small errors of judgment will become apparent and can be corrected next time. On the whole, gilding is best done in a cold room, without humidity. Cennini first drew attention to this in the 15th century.

Whichever way the frame has been gilded it needs a protective coat. This should not be a varnish like ormolu, which ruins the texture, although it might be needed in a bad atmosphere. Traditionally a thin glue size with water is used. It can be tinctured with a little water dye or aquarelle, or alternatively a yellow ochre or warm brown could be used.

A few drops of vernis ormolu emulsified in the size will make it more damp proof. The size should be very thin, a teaspoon (5 ml) of strong size to a quarter pint (150 ml) of warm water put on with a plant spray is satisfactory. This leaves no marks and the excess size can be stored in a jar and kept in a fridge for a couple of months. Animal glue, of which size is a refined and diffused derivative, is a strong and stable medium, used for tempera painting in the Renaissance and by Romans, Etruscans and Egyptians before that. Warm and wet or cold and jelled, it is quickly susceptible to bacteria which thrive on its protein, hence the need for storing in a fridge. Dry, it lasts for centuries. Use a spray as described earlier for the size, unless you are very confident about your deft, fast, even brushwork, which could lift the burnish.

Gilt frames in public collections have to be heavily protected and suffer a bit in consequence. Nevertheless it is worth while to study these, in their variety, exhaustively.

Some ornamented frames have a removable inset, a simple inner frame which is usually flat, with its sight edge bevelled or with a small spoon groove. These are usually gilded in matt gold, which must be perfect in its surface and must not be reflective as with burnishing, or uneven as with oil gold, which is used over variable surfaces. Two layers of leaf are laid, both bonded with very thin size over red bole. Smooth cavettoes or spoon grooves on for instance an Empire frame are usually matt gilded, similarly. The surface must be rubbed very smooth over the gesso. Very fine 'wet and dry' sandpaper, held on a wooden block, is useful. Then rub when dry with a piece of clean chamois. Sometimes it is useful to wet this, to eliminate micro scratches.

Make up some bole with the untallowed parchment size and rub smooth with chamois when dry. A little worn wet-and-dry paper might first be necessary. The surface must be flawless. Tilt the frame on a block and wet the higher end with a soft hog brush in cooled boiled water and lay the leaf when it is shiny wet. Cut the leaf so that it covers sections of the entire width each time and overlap slightly as you progress. At first it might be safer to do the edge groove separately in thin strips. Remove unstuck fragments of gold with a wet brush, but not overloaded, and fill in the faults, using only water since some size remains in the flecks of clay. When dry wipe down with cotton-wool. Apply a coat of weak, untallowed size to the gilded surface, allow it to dry and regild as before, using only water. Wipe it with cotton-wool when dry. Thin some untallowed size with one third of warm water and give the flat area two consecutive coats. The surface should be dull but lustrous and without faults. In framing as in any of the plastic arts, it is always more difficult to get a perfect surface. Fortunately it is not often desirable or necessary.

Wax

Wax is an important medium, superior in this context to all varnishes. The wax mixture used for the gold amalgam is very satisfactory. If the surface is polished with a piece of lambswool before the white spirit solvent has evaporated, some of the amalgam will rub off. So depending on the temperature wait for three to six hours before polishing.

Some antique furniture dealers and Alex Tiranti, the sculptors' suppliers, sell a micro-crystalline colourless wax polish in small tins. I recommend it heartily, a small amount goes a very long way for frames or furniture. Applied very thinly on a well-glasspapered, unfinished wooden moulding and then polished with lambswool. it gives a deep rich sheen and brings out a golden quality in the wood.

Plain wood should never be left plain since it becomes drab and dusty. Used over a spirit wood-stain of any hue, wax gives a sombre antique elegance. For a hint of colour on plain wood, paint on a thin wash of artists' water-colour and steel-wool the surface when dry, then wax. The tint will be minimal but very noticeable. Wax can also be used on gesso, textured or not. If the gesso is tinted with a pinch of yellow ochre and waxed, an appearance of ivory will emerge after wax polishing, and if a very thin wash of burnt umber and thin size is flooded on the cream-coloured cast and then wiped off the highlights before waxing, an antique ivory will result which will emphasize the modelling. In all cases, modelling patterns are strengthened by allowing a darker wash to deepen the hollows, leaving the highlights wiped cleaner. The colour for such washes consists, as mentioned before, of a touch of gouache, poster or dry pigment, mixed in thin size comprizing two tsp (10 g) of rabbit size to the quarter pint (150 ml) of water.

A useful and pleasing finish can be achieved on an ornamented frame or even a spoon moulding by staining the gesso to a light grey or similar pale neutral. If a cold tone is needed, add a speck of ultramarine blue to black and stir it into the gesso, a few grains at a time. Test on a scrap of wood and dry over heat, since the tone drops on drying. Yellow ochre, for instance, with black will produce a warm grey.

If the highlights of a tinted gessoed frame are touched with silver or gold amalgam, an otherwise drab frame can be agreeably adapted to a modern painting. Conversely a simple plain wood spoon or scooped moulding can be coated with a suitably tinted gesso (two coats) and the outer and inner ridges touched with a wax amalgam of silver or gold. This gives an agreeable but muted richness to an otherwise simple shape. This richness can be increased marginally by stippling the second layer of gesso. First paint on about 6 inches (150 mm) of gesso, wait for half a minute and then, holding the brush vertically, pounce the surface, raising hundreds of little bumps, one for every two or three hair ends. The colour and tone will be maintained but the tiny spots catch the light and give a pointillist luminosity to the carefully chosen neutral colour.

With care, using the thinnest smear of wax metal amalgam, it is even possible, by gently stroking the surface, to deposit a layer of metal on each of these tiny highlights. Burnish with an agate later. When touching ridges with wax metals, if there is any danger of the amalgam smearing on the surrounding areas, run masking tape on either side, pressed down lightly and removed immediately afterwards.

White frames

Maurice Denis (1870–1943), the 'Nabis' painter, describes the rise to fashion of white frames at the turn of the century, to absorb the more intense use of colour amongst his contemporaries, who were moving towards the violent colours of the 'Fauves'. Van Gogh wrote to his brother from Arles asking for white frames. All this makes visual sense, but by tinting and otherwise embellishing white gesso, a gentler harmony or contrast can be achieved in the same direction. Denis will be remembered by many painters and framers for his definition of a painting as an arrangement of colours on a flat surface, rather than an image of a landscape, a nude or a horse: an important point of departure when designing a frame. It was Edgar Degas (1834–1917), a particularly fastidious painter, who described the frame as the artist's reward; the end and the completion of the sweat and toil when the painting is seen as the artist intended, consciously or otherwise, from the first brushstroke.

REPAIR OF ORNAMENTED FRAMES

THE VAST MAJORITY of available ornamented frames are made of wood with added ornament in a chalky composition. Very shallow ornament is mechanically extruded onto modern frames, but rarely with any exuberance or quality. The frames considered here are likely to be from the 19th century. Generally speaking the earlier the better. The ornament from the late 18th century onwards was squeezed from moulds, usually carved in reverse in a close-grained wood, and there were regional variations in the casting medium.

A typical English 'compo' would consist of:

1 lb (0·5 kg) of scotch glue made thinly, mixed with 1 lb (0·5 kg) of pale resin boiled in half a pint (300 ml) raw linseed oil. Mix and sift in gilder's whiting (milled chalk). Blend to a stiff dough and either use shortly or dry into cakes. These can be softened by steam. A tin can in a pressure cooker for a quarter of an hour is convenient, though the hot dough or pasto is difficult to handle at first.

I would recommend a Spanish 'yeso' pasta as easier to make, particularly in small quantities, easily stored in a freezer. A similar gesso, using pulped paper, was used in Italy and France in the last quarter of the 18th century. It was a practice which infuriated people like Chippendale and Johnson because they saw it as cutting costs to the detriment of the product.

To make a gesso (It.) or Yeso (Sp.) pasta, put some gilder's whiting in a bowl, (a typical amount might be 4 heaped tbsp/90 ml). Add a quarter in bulk of pulped newsprint. Rub together to break up the pulp and add some thin rabbit glue, stir and knead. If too soggy, add more whiting. A stiff dough results, which should be alternately rolled into a ball, rolled between the palms into a sausage shape, patted into a ball again and so forth, several times. It is not ready for use yet, and at this stage it can be stored in a freezer for months and a fridge for weeks.

Either rabbit glue or pearl glue can be used to make gesso pasta, but the extra flexibility of rabbit glue, normally used to make rabbit size, is no particular advantage when binding a dense mass. Pearl glue is derived from cattle and should be soaked in water before it can be used, in the same way as rabbit glue. They are both forms of gelatine and are first cousins of the familiar flavoured table jelly. They are both stocked by theatrical colour merchants or gilders' suppliers, and need to soak in cold water for three or four hours before being melted down by heating.

For the gesso pasta, shake five generous teaspoonfuls (about 40 ml) in a quarter pint (150 ml) of cold water in a bean tin or something similar. Stand in about 2 inches (5 cm) boiling water in a pan until liquid, then stir and use. The surplus can be stored in a fridge. When

The broken corner of a frame on which a sound corner remains. The ornament is cut back to a logical point

The missing part is replaced and tidied up with polyfilla. The gesso paste 'squeezed' from the silicone mould is similar to the piece incorporated

A cast of a sound corner of the frame in silicone rubber. Alginate casting powder would do the job, but this is a useful ornament to keep for future use

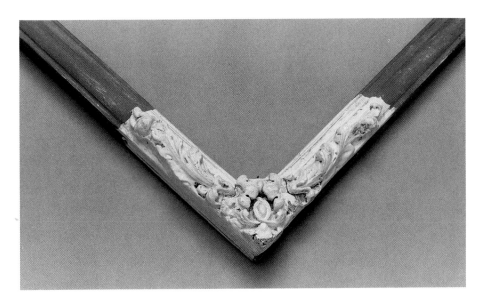

A sound corner from which a flexible cast can be made to replace the missing piece

The repaired frame treated with red bole and rubbed smooth for gilding

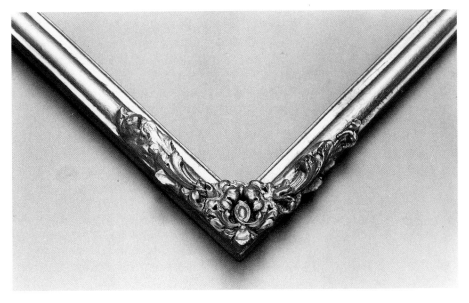

The repaired frame, gessoed, painted in red bole and gilded. In this case with burnishing bronze in size and wax amalgam burnished

Small repairs with Alginate powder. The outer beading has been done already and now the high torus moulding is greased for casting

Water is added to the alginate which is very rapidly spread and pressed on to a section of moulding

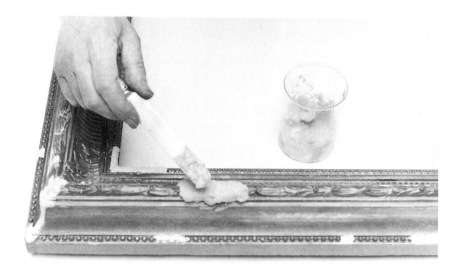

wet all animal gels are natural forcing beds for bacteria. When dry they become inert. Seal when in the fridge to avoid loss of water.

Paper is pulped by tearing it into postage stamp sized pieces, a quick process when torn in wads. Soak for half an hour in warm water. Add some bleach for the ink if inclined, but wash out in a sieve afterwards. Put back into warm water and roll between the palms of the hand until it breaks into a coarse porridge. It can then be put through a liquidizer with added water, judging suitable amounts, and tipped into a sieve to drain. It doesn't harm the liquidizer, but alternatively it can be rolled on a concrete doorstep, in a soggy wet state, to a suitably fine pulp. Place back in more water, stir and drain through a sieve. In either case, drop it into a cloth and squeeze out much of the excess water. Break it up by hand and store in a sealed jar indefinitely. A honey pot full will be enough for a large amount of gesso pasta.

So much for the raw material for a piece of conservation, but the repairs themselves vary to an enormous degree. If they consist of tiny chips of white here and there, they can be filled with a cellulose

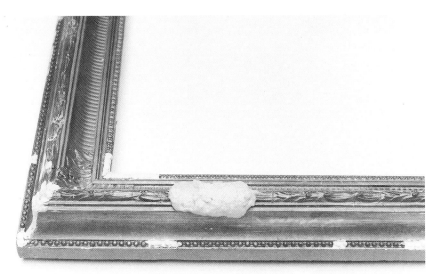

The alginate lump should be pressed down until it gels to ensure fine detail

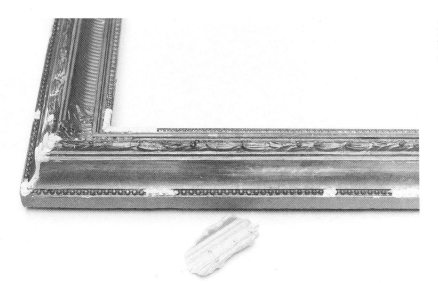

After about 3 runs the cast can be removed. Because the ornament lies on the flat it can be cast in Crystacal and glued down when dry

plaster filler like Polyfilla, rubbed smooth and treated as described later. It is possible however to restore excellently even when the frame looks a complete wreck, without, for instance, even one complete corner ornament remaining. In this case, the entirely missing piece must be remodelled in clay on to the broken piece and the entire piece cast in silicone rubber. Four casts in gesso pasta can then be built onto the frame, but this is an extreme case, usually at least one corner or similar piece of ornament remains.

Build a makeshift shoulder around the corner or centre ornament, on the outside only, and brush a thin coat of petroleum jelly over the area to be cast. Make a silicone rubber mould as described earlier, remove it and replace it. Oil its back and put a half-inch (12-mm) thick layer of plaster over the oiled area with a flat knife, where possible a half inch (12 mm) in from the edge. A rigid plaster case is needed so that the gesso pasta or composition can be pressed into the mould. Often the repair is a missing section of torus (half-circle cross section) border from $\frac{3}{4}$–$\frac{1}{4}$ inch (19–6 mm) in width. Such ornaments always lie on a flat surface so can be cast in Crystacal and fixed in the

A flexible mould of a corner ornament in a plaster base

Oil the mould and feed in the gesso paste from a logical starting point

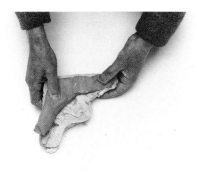

Press in using the thumbs until it is filled and level

gap or gaps with a contact adhesive. If the cast is too thick it must be rubbed thinner on a file or sandpaper.

While silicone rubber moulds are extremely accurate and cast well, a one- or two-off flexible mould can be made with an alginate casting powder, a sort of plaster with a vegetable gelling substance mixed in it. Tiranti sell 'Scopas Alginate' in airtight packets and a similar material has been used for dental casting for many years. Mixed half-and-half with water, it must be spread on a greased surface immediately, since it sets within a couple of minutes. It should be used, lightly oiled, as soon as possible because it deteriorates rapidly, though its life can be prolonged for three or four days by sealing it in a plastic bag in a fridge, not a freezer. In emergencies for very small repairs, a mould can be made from body-warm plasticene pressed down on the surface with a flat piece of wood to give it a flat back to lie on without modulations. If this is chilled in a fridge it becomes very hard and will withstand some pressure, and will not readily become pasty when lightly oiled. It should remain however an occasional minor makeshift.

If a gesso pasta squeeze or pressing is taken from a silicone mould and allowed to dry hard, it will come away easily. Since however the main purpose of gesso pasta is to remove it when it is wet and flexible, the mould should be lightly oiled to open the vacuum. Raw linseed oil is best, brushed in and the surplus wiped off. In an emergency, cooking oil will serve.

The gesso pasta described above is traditional and serviceable, but an accidental (or inspired) discovery by a lazy but intelligent ex-student of mine is a great improvement. Take a lump of the pasta sufficient for about twenty minutes' work, a tin of the same warm thin rabbit glue or rich size, and a heap of Crystacal to equal the pasta in bulk. Dab the pasta in the Crystacal and work in whatever sticks, with the palms of the hand. It will become a little dry and friable but if dunked in the warm glue and rerolled and dabbed in the mound of Crystacal again, will regain its sticky doughlike texture.

This can be repeated until all the Crystacal is taken up. Roll, squash and reroll until a ductable mass is achieved. Tear off a lump and roll it on a folded newspaper into a thick snake or sausage and, starting at one end, or corner of the mould, press it in with the thumbs, moving progressively along. Keep the surface as even as possible and tear off any surplus that happens at the end. If too little has been used, add some more, not at the unfinished end, but a little distance back, amalgamating the addition to the main mass.

Having previously cleaned up the surface on to which the fragment of design is to be laid, by chipping off extraneous lumps, dab on some of the still warm rabbit glue thinly, and before it gels, smear on the thinnest skin of gesso pasta, working it down firmly and rapidly so that it clings. Take the filled mould from its plaster bed, turn it opening downwards on a piece of newspaper, bend it slightly from one end, corner or extremity. The cast should fall out by its own weight, face up. If it is very deep, a little levering with a small screwdriver or spatula at some point will encourage this fall. Give a flick of the warm rabbit glue (or thick size) to the thin skin of pasta on the wood and the bottom part of the released cast and lay the cast in place without delay, pressing down very carefully to avoid squashing it. Press down into hollows if possible, using a small spatula. Trim and fudge the junction points between old and new ornament, but stop short of injuring the soft new cast. Joints can be sandpapered and fudged over with Polyfilla when dry.

Very large extending corner ornaments need supporting underneath their overlay. Sometimes a couple of nails on the edge of the corner will act as a cantilever beam, but occasionally a loop of heavy wire can be epoxy-resined into two holes to act as a support. When dry, the supports can be covered with more gesso pasta underneath and softened down into the sides of the corner. The repaired frame will look like a half-chewed dog biscuit when dry and trimmed. Rub down the repairs with some 000 steel wool and brush clean until you have studied the finishing techniques described earlier.

There are available in some art shops and sculptors' suppliers epoxy resin modelling materials (e.g. Milliput). These consist of an epoxy resin and separate hardening agent, both made up to a malleable paste capable of fine moulding, self adhesion and hardness. Kneaded together these can be squeezed in a mould or modelled directly. They are very useful and crisp for small repairs, in particular, narrow ridges or the corner of a broken leaf and the like. To attach, first make a wet mud of a fragment and work it onto the broken surface. The stiffer bulk will bond to this without destructive pressure. It can be chiselled or filed to an often essential sharpness, and is useful for deep cracks and small repairs. Liquid gesso is more suitable for shallow depressions and hair cracks, being softer for smoothing.

For the repair of a totally missing and repeated pattern area on an ornamented frame, it has to be modelled in the same style. Sometimes a piece can be taken from another frame and reproduced. It will not be the same as the original but, carefully chosen from the same idiom, it may serve just as well, whether it be a corner ornament or a border moulding. The finished frame should be consistent. If remodelling is needed, plasticene, wax or clay can be used. I find clay easiest. After rough modelling it can be carved crisp when cheese dry. If it is intricate, make an intermediary mould in dental plaster and after cleaning, crispen it with a small chisel or sharpened screwdriver. Oil the mould and take a clay squeeze. This will give a very sharp result, which can itself be sharpened further, if it seems necessary.

At this point I am addressing people with some modelling skill. Before starting, examine the linear logic of the existing part of the

Remove the rubber mould from the case; turn face downwards and pick at the corner of the cast with a small tool; peel off the cast when it flops down

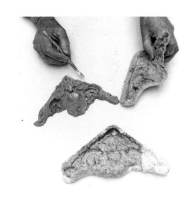

The soggy cast should be glued in the frame within about 15 minutes

Thin casts and newly modelled ornaments are laid on well-secured wire supports and filled in behind with fresh composition or pasta. This is then trimmed when dry for finishing

Baroque and rococo mouldings are not
formed from simple repeating patterns and
cannot be mitred just anywhere. To decrease
a length, remove a suitable unit of design,
possibly two, and rejoin the rest. To
lengthen, cut the design and insert newly
cast units and tidy up

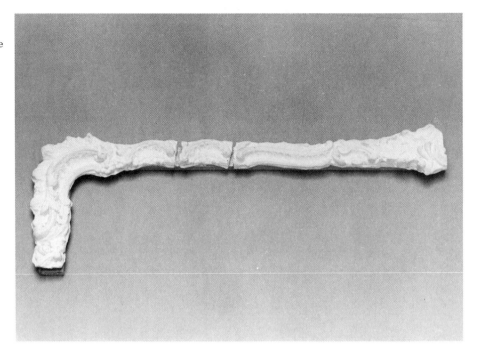

design, the structure of a C scroll or acanthus leaf, and make a line drawing of its curves and symmetries. It need not be an accomplished drawing, merely a guide to structure which will make the modelling easier. Sometimes this modelling can be done on the broken area of frame, using a couple of nail pins to support it if necessary.

If it is very extensive, cast the sound area in alginate or silicone rubber, take a clay 'squeeze' of the right thickness, lay it flat on a board and the new area can be fashioned on to it with greater ease. Remould the clay entirely in silicone rubber and not only will it enable the frame to be repaired but it can be kept for further use in refabricating injured frames of a similar kind and for making new ones. This has been mentioned before in a different context, but is worth repeating more specifically.

There are a few points to remember when taking a cast from a sound section of a frame to replace a missing or badly damaged section. Always make the flexible mould from an area of design slightly larger than the one you wish to replace. Clear the missing or broken area to some logical point in the pattern. Do not try to subdivide a flower cluster or a piece of fussy strapwork, but chisel it off the wood, leaving space for a coherent area of design as self-sufficient as possible. Only common sense can decide. Before taking a 'squeeze' in gesso pasta or composition make a 'squeeze' in modelling clay or warm plasticene and lay it near you as a reference to the design pattern, which is sometimes difficult to 'read' in reverse in the mould with any accuracy. An eye judgment can then be made as to where to trim the gesso pasta insert so that it fits in snugly, joining on to where it should. Lay the gesso 'squeeze' on the table and cut it to size with a sharp thin knife. Make sure it is the right thickness, which is apparent if it is laid in place temporarily. If not, take a second squeeze. Often the same lump of gesso pasta can be used, but dunk it again into the size and reroll it between the hands.

MAKING ANTIQUE FRAMES FROM DRAWINGS OR PHOTOGRAPHS

FOR THOSE WITH any facility in modelling, any running patterns can be copied. Most ornamented mouldings consist of single unit of pattern, perhaps 3 or 4 inches (75–100 mm) long, repeated indefinitely. No particular attempt is usually made to align a pattern at a corner, as when hanging wall paper, since this might well involve cutting the sides too long or too short.

When making home-made decorated mouldings, ingenuity can be used to fudge certain ornate patterns by a little subtraction from the pattern on one side with a small chisel and a little rebuilding on the other side of the corner with epoxy putty or gesso pasta. This can be rubbed down and sharpened on drying so that the pattern appears to run around the corner on the finished frame, but in fact does not.

In ornament, the eye is more easily deceived than with austere mouldings or parallel ridges and spooned sections. Alternatively, a suitable corner ornament can be added whenever the design allows. Sometimes this is not desirable, since certain paintings demand a rectangular profile, and corner ornaments themselves vary so much in opulence and relative simplicity that care in choice is needed. Sometimes a small corner ornament can be used on a frame not extending beyond its outer profile. Roundel ornaments which can sometimes be taken from old pieces of furniture were sometimes used in the 19th century and earlier. These, as the name suggests, are

This flowing pattern meets uneasily at the corners. By cutting away and building up with gesso paste, polyfilla or epoxy putty, a continuous mitreless flow results

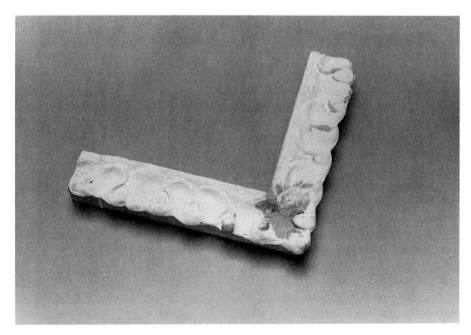

Previous Pages.
Left (*underneath*): A Spanish Baroque frame;
(*on top*) An art deco frame with doctored
corners

Right: A copy of a Nicholas Hilliard
(*c.* 1547–1619) miniature in enamel on copper.
The rather spiky strapwork frame was
common in northern Europe in Tudor times

round ornaments rather like carved draughtsmen or rosettes. Dante Gabriel Rossetti designed several with his private esoteric symbols for some of his frames. Corner ornaments which derive from the baroque and the rococo styles were not devised to cover an untidy corner, but they certainly have that effect in practice.

The example I have chosen for producing a frame from drawings, line sketches taken in a gallery, or from photographs is Spanish baroque. My reasons are threefold. It is a gracious type of frame, like much else in Spanish design, austere yet sensual. The fine elements to which I have reduced it are simple to model with no intricacy of C scrolls or artificial foliage, and it is an extremely usable design for portraits and much else and would be more widely used if it were more readily available. It is rare to find one in antique galleries or auctions and they are not very common in public collections either. Even in the Rastro flea market in Madrid where they could once be seen now and then, they have virtually disappeared, probably into dealers' stocks.

All Spanish baroque frames are slightly different. A style of frame is not like a model of a car, where each one is identical. What they share is a style, a proportion and a common rhythm of ornament. Gothic cathedrals are very different from each other, but they share common recognizable qualities. Art Deco cinema design, now being reappraised, varied from high street to high street, but there was a common style, recognizable from the top of a bus in a snowstorm. So it is with frames in a given style. The example given here has been shorn of certain exuberances, but not very much, and this is quite allowable.

Like most baroque frames, there are emphatic corner ornaments and centre ornaments and a running (repeated) inner and outer border. Sometimes one or the other of these border strips is wider or a little more elaborate, but not much and not always. I am concerned here with shapes that can be formed easily. Anyone who can, is welcome to elaborate. The illustration shows a couple of working sketches

A corner adjusted by modelling a continuous
flow of ornament

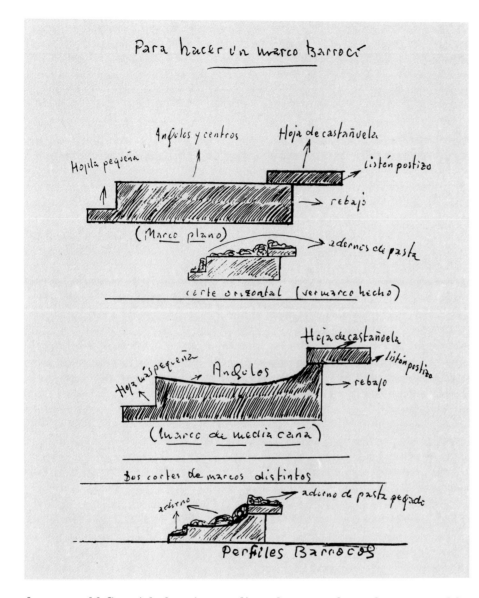

from an old Spanish framing atelier, the sort of rough note used by framers for centuries, sometimes scribbled by the artist. Examples by Rembrandt and Constable exist. Thousands must have been used to light pipes or stoves. These show the slightly variable profiles of Spanish baroque and the proportions can be modified to taste.

Few shapes are simpler to assemble: it is just three strips of wood glued together, all flat, to which ornament is added. This consists of four corner ornaments, which in this Italian-style frame do not break the rectangular outer profile. There are two centre ornaments of different sizes, one for the short sides and one for the longer; it is not essential to have both, although together they allow finer control of visual weight; by using only the smaller one a smaller, uncrowded frame can be made. Quite a lot of the surface of a Spanish baroque frame is plain, usually of a dark colour. The outer and inner wooden strips, one forming the rebate, are decorated with a running strip of abstract repeated ornament, both simple but different. I will deal with these first.

Both consist of a repeated motif, one of two modified rectangles

Various frame ornaments, including baroque, rococo and classical

A glazed frame with gold intaglio tiles to echo a Mogul painting

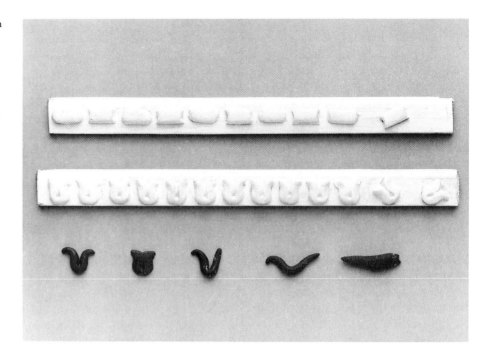

Top: A Spanish baroque assembling pattern for an outer border, made with casts from silicone mould of original clay model

Centre: A similar assembling of an inner border

Bottom: The metamorphosis of a unit shape from a piece of modelling clay

A silicone rubber mould of the outer and inner borders of the moulding

and the other a keyhole or omega shape, as shown. Shape the two-rectangle unit in clay on a piece of glass to a chosen size: stick two strips of masking tape the required width apart and exactly parallel on the back of the glass. Model the clay shapes on the top side, guided by the tapes. Form a small silicone mould from the two rectangles, which are treated as one unit. Model the omega shape on glass from a worm of clay, tapering at both ends, and bend and mould it on the glass. Two or three tries may be necessary to get a tapering worm of the right length. The edges must be at an angle of 90° or slightly less, to the glass base to avoid undercuts. With a rubber mould a degree of undercutting is allowable, but in this case it is not necessary. A crisp edge in any modelling gives a greater illusion of hollowness or undercutting. This is then cast in silicone rubber, at the same time as the first. It is easier and more economic to cast several units at the same time.

This part of the job can be done at odd moments over several days. These units are then cleaned and rubber cemented onto glass along a taped-down strip of wood used as a straight-edge which is removed on completion. The strips are best formed up to about 3 feet (1 m) long, convenient for storing in a cupboard, the ultimate criterion. It is quicker to use the more rapid-setting dental plaster for such casting since it halves the waiting time, and no great hardness is needed for the pattern. A silicone rubber mould is made of these casts, just as if they were part of a frame moulding.

The very abstract designs of the corner and centre ornaments derive from a vegetable pattern. Much of Greco Roman architectural design was semi-abstracted from natural leaves, acanthus, laurel, ivy and so forth, originally symbols of gods: ivy for Dionysius, laurel for Apollo. These became increasingly conventionalized so that an 'artificial' leaf became in architects' or framers' parlance an exact formal thing.

Examples of this are very useful when analyzing frame mouldings. By the late 17th century the full flowering of baroque led to wild and, it must be said, agreeable abstraction. It is difficult at times to recognize the interlaced strapwork on a Louis IV frame as rarefied foliage.

The corner and centre ornaments on Spanish baroque frames vary greatly but all are recognizable as such. They must be of the same width throughout and this can be done by modelling them on glass with parellel bands of tape on the under side, as a guide. It is safer, however, to draw out the general structure of the design on mount board and cut out the pieces with a knife or scissors. Cement these onto glass or smooth hardboard and model on top of them. When drawing, a simple black outline of the main masses is enough and a pair of compasses or dividers ensures the balanced dimensions of similar shapes facing in two different directions. It is not a lengthy job and is closer to pattern making than what is normally considered modelling. Make two or three silicone rubber moulds of the pieces and they are ready to use.

A Chinese cartouche ornament modelled in clay from a drawn pattern using hand-made spatulas

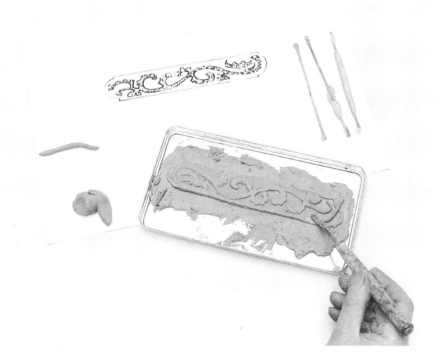

Far left: A Renaissance pattern resembling a Persian border, and used for a mogul painting

The pattern from a Chinese urn finished like ivory. The mount is in raw silk

A Neo-gothic moulding adapted from a frame in the National Gallery, Edinburgh

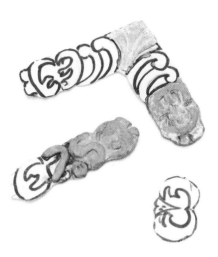

Above: A Spanish baroque modelling ornament in clay on a pattern drawn on thick card

Below: A silicone rubber mould

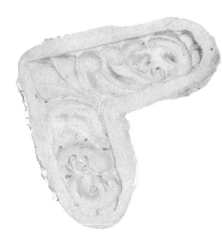

Casts in Crystacal

In this sort of modelling I find that the spatulas available in art shops are not convenient, being more suitable for larger heads, figures or whatever. Some can be pared thinner to give a more blade-like effect, which is the most useful. There is more paring, scraping and 'carving' than usual and the desired result must be smooth and crisp.

Tools can be made from nails and pieces of thick wire (such as old coat hangers). Cut the head from a 4-inch (100-mm) nail and heat one end red hot. As quickly as possible, beat it with a hammer until about $\frac{1}{2}$–$\frac{3}{4}$ inches (12–19 mm) of it broadens out to a spade, this does not take long. Hammer until the 'blade' is a little thicker than needed and then file it to a rounded paddle shape and smooth both sides, finishing them off with emery paper. Six inches (150 mm) of heavy gauge wire will make a double-ended tool of different sized 'blades' or one with a flat chisel-like tip, useful for clearing surfaces. Steel-wool the metal to a fine polish and roughen the shanks with a file. A thickening of epoxy putty or plastic wood will make a handle or grip for the fingers, useful when twirling and turning the spatula when working the clay, plasticene or wax. After modelling, a square hog brush, dipped in water, is useful for smoothing out the surface. It becomes a useful tool for cleaning out hollows where unwanted clay rubble tends to collect. When wet, the highlights can be rubbed smooth with the forefinger. This is usually frowned on in more conventional modelling, but we are dealing here with very elaborate pattern making.

A set of such tools can be made in less than an afternoon, apart from the drying time for the plastic wood or epoxy putty, but they will last a lifetime, though they are readily stolen and easily lost.

While it has nothing to do with the immediate subject, such tools, shaped to whim and experience, are useful for modelling medallions, medals and the like, which indeed can occur on specially designed frames. In lighter moments with students, we have designed frames with dogs' heads, cats' heads, human portraits and Chinese dragons as corner ornaments for frame follies, often for unusual mirror glass frames, and they never fail to stimulate conversation and give pleasure. It is not uncommon to have to copy or forge an eagle or a crest of some sort on a mirror glass frame. If the mass of the modelling looks like being too heavy, coat the inside of the mould with Crystacal $\frac{1}{4}$ inch (6 mm) thick with a brush, and when partly set, lay in strips of medium or coarse jute scrim (not the cotton stuff like bandage) and paint some more Crystacal through the scrim to cement it into the structure, overlapping it slightly.

Two short rods (sawn-off nails) can be incorporated into the casting or dowelled in later, at its base, to slot into a block fixed behind the frame. Fibrous casts can be both strong and light.

Only the narrow outer and inner borders of the Spanish baroque frame are 'running' or repeated units of the same pattern. The corners and centre designs are discontinuous with plain areas between.

The Gothic frame illustrated here was adapted from a frame in the Scottish National Gallery, Edinburgh. Gothic revival was very popular in the mid-19th century, exemplified by Pugin's decorative additions to the Westminster Houses of Parliament or in France by the mediaeval recreations of Viollet le Duc. The phrase may have been originally an expression of the Oxford Movement, or more probably the last kick of the Romantic epoch when Ivanhoe was a world hero from Milan to Boston.

Some Gothic frames were very spiky, with fretted finials and crockets resembling the skyline of Lincoln Cathedral. The Edinburgh frame was quattrocento in its simplicity: a broad central flat with a plain narrow outer and inner border with a repeated double ogee design in relief along the central flat. The copy or adaptation described was devised to frame some small landscapes, dark and mysterious, which seemed suitable for hanging in Schloss Frankenstein.

The flat frame was quattrocento in style, one unit of this double ogee tracery was drawn, carefully centred so that it could be accurately joined to cast duplicates and cut out in mounting board. The clay was modelled on this and cast in silicone rubber. Casts were taken from this in quick-setting dental plaster and joined together, glued to a board and tidied up. A silicone mould was then taken of the assembly and set in a bed as described earlier. Frail to handle when cast, it became strong when glued to the wooden flat of the moulding.

Such designs are soft in contour and easy to model. More detailed units of pattern should first be modelled and cast in plaster. Make a little clay wall around the unit and pour in dental plaster in a thin creamy state, always adding plaster to water and pouring off the surplus 'whey'. Tap to remove air bubbles. The reverse shape can then be crispened with small tools, sharpened small screwdrivers, chisels made by hammering the end of nails, filing and sharpening. A squeeze can then be taken from the oiled mould with clay, and mounted on a board and reproduced as earlier. If the pull is difficult to extract (its back must be smooth), fill the mould with an epoxy putty and chip away the mould when the cast has hardened, not forgetting to grease it first. A variety of Renaissance patterns, undulates, grecos etc., can be contrived in this way. Irregular shapes can be reversed by first modelling and casting and then making a paper template of the cast and turning it upside down to get the exact outline for the reverse.

Any inventive framer can extend this technology as needs demand given, as should be, a reasonable knowledge of art history or books of reference. Museums are a prime source. The Chinese frame was taken from a bronze Ming ritual vessel (1368–1643), a unit of the repeating design being copied in a sketchbook by the showcase and redrawn to actual scale in line on thin paper. The background was an even ribbon of clay on a board crosshatched with a nail and a set square. A similar ribbon of clay was levelled on a talced board to prevent sticking and the shape marked through the paper outline with a fine ballpoint. It was then cut free from the rest of the clay, with a small knife, tidied up, moistened on the back and laid on the moistened crosshatched ribbon and pressed down. Finer detail was then modelled or carved on the design. A silicone mould was made of this and half a dozen plaster casts taken. These were carefully stuck to a strip of glass and the pattern smoothed and sharpened by carving. The joints were patched with soft plaster and the background crosshatched with an awl and a sliding set-square, a technique used on gesso on neo-rococo 19th-century frames, but accurate in this case.

A silicone rubber mould was then taken of the finished pattern and a transparent green-blue glaze finish using an epoxy resin was used to give an oriental-style appearance.

In the search for 'ethnic' designs for adaptation to a frame moulding the field is wide, depending on one's perspicacity.

An eagle mirror glass crest in hollow reinforced Crystacal, which is light and strong

OVAL, BOX, FLOATING, AND TRAY, LUNETTE GEORGIAN PRINT FRAMES

OVAL FRAMES

VASARI DESIGNED some oval frames for the Medicis in the 16th century, but their popularity increased in the 17th and 18th centuries, usually with a few C scrolls added. Watteau shows them in his shop sign for the dealer Gersaint, and towards the end of the century there was a revival, with neo-classical additions, before the French Revolution. They are rare in English records.

All of these would have been large, 3 or 4 feet (91 or 122 cm) high, carved in sections in wood and joined together. Today large oval frames are used rarely, if at all, by painters, and small ones are made in Italy, cut in wood by an ingenious lathe for the photographic trade, but even this practice is dying out. The vignetted oval photo portraits of the first decades of this century have been replaced by rectangular colour prints.

There are two ways to frame an oval picture of any size, be it in oil on canvas board (canvases on stretchers are rectangular), a wooden panel or anything else.

A spandrelled frame is rectangular with an oval or a round opening. They were in vogue from the latter part of the 18th century to the middle of the 19th century. The outer frame can be made in the manner described earlier, with a fairly narrow moulding. The centre is cut from plywood or hardboard to the correct oval proportion. The painting shown is really a compressed sphere rather than a geometrical oval. The four corners are the spandrels, an architectural term, and were always decorated like a grandfather clock face.

The four spandrel ornaments, typical of this kind of frame, can either be modelled in clay from some reference source and cast in silicone rubber and then Crystacal (it lies on a flat surface), or taken from part of a corner ornament from a rococo frame. Some imaginative ingenuity is called for.

The rebate, which is also the inner border, is a narrow Boule moulding cast in gesso pasta and bent around the curve in sections. A little fudging was needed at the joints. Since the rebate was impossibly shallow, it was deepened from behind with a discontinuous oval of blocks made from pieces of one-by-one (25×25 mm) glued on. A variety of mouldings and ornaments, classical, some baroque and more rococo, can be combined in constructing a spandrelled frame of this kind, depending on occasion and opportunity. Access to old frames for taking silicone moulds is naturally important.

A purely oval frame of any size can be 'run' in gesso on a core. 'Running' consists of painting or carefully pouring gesso over a core of wood and pulling over this a template cut in metal. In the first few 'runnings', moving the template over the partly covered core, only

Far right: A copy of a Tudor miniature (enamel on copper) in a spandrelled 19th-century frame. It is a Crystacal cast on wood and gilded larger spandrelled frames have much richer ornament

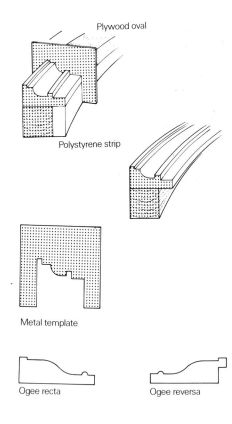

Plywood oval

Polystyrene strip

Metal template

Ogee recta

Ogee reversa

'Running' an oval or round (tondo) frame. During the running a polystyrene strip fills the rebate area

key points will be scraped to the right profile, but gradually, painting on more gesso each time and cleaning up the side dribbles, the exact profile is cut in the gesso. Any residual roughness can be cleaned off with sandpaper. Traditionally, the core was a winding of strips of wood veneer glued on both sides, wound around a palisade of moulding pins less than $\frac{1}{4}$ inch (6 mm) apart, tapped into the desired oval drawn on a flat wooden base. The width or height of the core depended on the size of the template profile, allowing at least $\frac{1}{8}$ inch (3 mm) clearance for the gesso at the narrowest point.

It is a slow process with delays between each separate scraping of the template. When it is completed, the entirety is prised off the board, the points of the moulding pins filed off or tapped flat and the rebate cut out with a sharp knife and a small chisel. This last part is not so difficult, since the windings of laminated veneer strip break off fairly easily. This same process, apart from the core, has been used for centuries for making ceiling cornice mouldings in plaster: a messy, upside down job, manipulated from the top of a ladder.

It is possible to simplify this process, either with gesso, or more quickly with Crystacal, by externalizing the core. By this I mean cutting, or having cut, an oval hoop of plywood on a bandsaw, a $\frac{1}{4}$ inch (6 mm) narrower than the chosen size of the moulding or its metal reverse profile. If the moulding is 2 inches (50 mm) wide, the bandsaw oval should be $1\frac{3}{4}$ inches (45 mm) so that the overhanging moulding, shaped by the template, forms a rebate when glued onto it.

In cutting the metal profile, make sure that it is rigid. A section of a strong can is useful for this, but if it is flexible screw an inverted U of $\frac{1}{4} \times \frac{1}{4}$-inch (6 × 6-mm) wood around its outside to ensure rigidity. In choosing a profile, take a look in galleries and make some notes. Something involving an ogee or a cavetto (scooped) shape is best, or at least easier, and gives sufficient emphasis. The profile should be drawn on paper, with the thickness of the plywood oval taken into account. Thus, to complete the drawing for transferring to the piece of metal, the depth of the plywood oval should be added. Furthermore, the profile of the face should be drawn at least $\frac{1}{4}$ inch (6 mm) wider than the plywood oval to give an overhang to form a rebate when the finished moulding is 'run' and glued to the plywood. If the frame is larger than 18 inches (455 mm) high, allow more. Cut a trial template in cardboard and test it over the ply oval; redesign it if the rebate overhang is too thin or shallow to be strong enough. It should be between $\frac{1}{8}$ inch (3 mm) and $\frac{1}{4}$ inch (6 mm) depending on size. Now cut some strips of polystyrene foam ceiling tiles or package filling and glue these to the inside of the plywood oval to fill the space where the rebate should be, out to the inside edge of the template. Lightly cement the oval with its polystyrene addition to a smooth board, possibly plastic laminated, and sandpaper the whole shape smooth so that it exactly fits the template.

Lightly but thoroughly grease the extended oval and its base with petroleum jelly, and complete the metal template, having modified its contour from the cardboard try-out if necessary, as it nearly always is.

Mix enough Crystacal to cover the oval about $\frac{1}{4}$ inch (6 mm) deep. The addition of a few squeezes of PVA wood glue to the water will help to slow the setting and harden the ultimate result. Start 'running' the template along the gentler curve of the oval first, but ensuring that at all times the template is at right angles to the plywood and stays vertical. It must not be allowed to slope wideways. This requires some concentration at the shorter curves at top and bottom. Wipe off any surplus Crystacal extruded onto the base or the template and lay it on the face if it is still soft and workable, discard it if not. Quite possibly, traces of the cutting profile will begin to show in discontinuous spots at the first 'running'. Continue the process, pouring or brushing some more Crystacal onto the uncut areas and scraping it into shape. As the profile nears completion, use thinner Crystacal. The finished shape can be cleaned down with wet and dry paper when wet and glasspapered when dry.

Lever the whole thing, plywood oval as well, off the wooden base: the reason for cementing it down lightly, just enough to hold it. If it does not come easily, immerse it or flood it with water for a few minutes, which will break the glue seal. Remove the Crystacal from the plywood by judicious levering with a knife. It should lift easily from the greased surface. If the polystyrene strips cling to the Crystacal, pick them off and trim the rebate with a small chisel.

Dry the plywood oval, remove all trace of the petroleum jelly with mineral spirit (white spirit) and cement it to the Crystacal with a contact adhesive and sandpaper the outer edge.

Quite a lot of cleaning, sizing, and gessoing are needed to finish, but this is done using the techniques described earlier, according to need or taste.

Three-dimensional objects, low reliefs, medallions, coins, necessitate a modification of conventional framing. In effect the frame has to become a shallow showcase with a separation of plus or minus an inch (25 mm) between the glass and the base board on which the object lies.

The thickness or depth of the frame is a matter of choice or convenience, but it should not be too narrow, since the objects are likely to have a degree of visual as well as actual weight. The example illustrated is largely made of two-by-one (50 × 25 mm) timber, finished. This means about $1\frac{3}{4} \times \frac{3}{4}$ inches (45 × 19 mm). Cut the four sides straight, not mitred, and glue a flat strip $\frac{1}{10}$ inch (2·5 mm) from the top and $\frac{1}{4}$ inch (6 mm) from the bottom. This will make a rebate on top for the glass and at the bottom for the piece of suitably covered hardboard on which the object is fixed. Sometimes a few dabs of suitable glue will be enough for this, sometimes a few staples made from floral wire can be pushed through two tiny holes and taped down behind to hold them. The flat side strip that forms the rebates might well be covered in the same way as the base board: possibly a fabric, fixed with a fabric glue aerosol spray.

The top, where the glass rests in its rebate groove, should be capped with a fluted flat strip a little wider than the piece of finished two-by-one (50 × 25 mm) about 1 inch (25 mm) wide. These four strips should not be glued to the rest of the box, until the four sides of the box, with their double rebates, are mitred and assembled. This done, the glass is laid in place and the four strips of fluted moulding should be tapped into place with moulding pins, about three on each side. These should be punched in and the hollow filled. If the glass breaks it is easy to prise off these fluted mouldings and replace the glass and the mouldings. The back base is held in place by pins, sealed with gummed tape, and the box frame can be suitably finished. This could be achieved by a coat of dark spirit stain and wax polish with its suggestion of a Georgian bookcase, to gilding, silvering or texturing with gesso in any of the ways previously described.

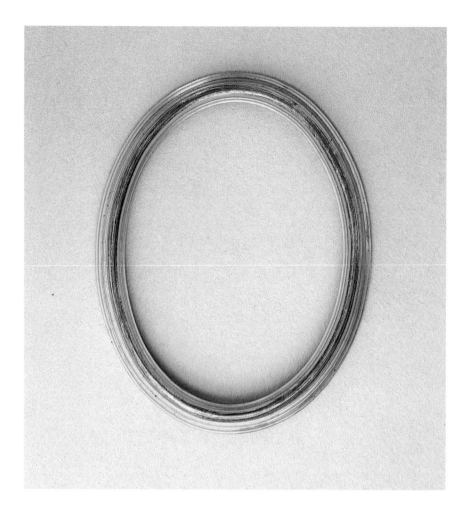

A plain oval frame, used mostly for
photographs from 1890–1918

A small corner ornament gives a simple
stained moulding the feeling of period, as if
from an old country house library

This frame isolates the drawing like a painting hanging on a textured screen or wall. At the same time it fulfils the conventions of framing

A lunette frame for an 18th-century fan (small model)

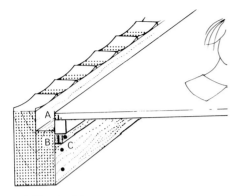

A 'floating' frame serves to isolate a painting. Some Paul Klee paintings have variants of this

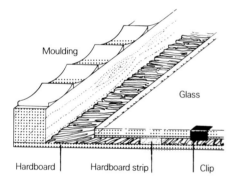

A 'tray' frame gives quiet isolation with emphatic presentation to line drawings etc

FLOATING FRAMES

An effective way to frame certain small canvases, say up to 20×30 inches (510×750 mm) or thereabouts, is to surround the bare canvas on its stretcher with a shallow trough of darkness which gives an unusual isolation to the painting. The illustrations give an idea of how this can be achieved. The frame should be deep and any ornament should be unemphatic. The purpose is to induce a deep shadow between the canvas edge, which should be dark, and the inside of A, also darkened, shrouding the top of B, also darkened, in a rim of deep shadow.

The wood needed is a matter of choice, but it could consist of two-by-one (50×25 mm) (A), $1\frac{1}{4} \times 1$ inch (30×25 mm) (B) and one-by-one (25×25 mm) (C). The trough between canvas and A could be covered in dark fabric, but stippled gesso painted with a suitable dark tempera or acrylic colour is probably as good for light absorption and easier to do. The face of the frame is the top of A. A light decorated moulding, ornamented or in wood, can be glued here, but probably textured gesso is enough. With a dark tempera wash, the gesso-textured highlights can be touched with gold or silver amalgam. Quite a number of the paintings of Paul Klee are framed in this way, often with adapted and old ornamented frames. Both he and his heirs had the same finesse of vision that he displayed in his painting.

TRAY FRAMES

An elegant and useful way of framing something light and precious, a drawing, a flat collage or some such, can be done as illustrated. I used it once for a small 17th-century Jesuit map of the canals and ponds of Pekin which had no beginning or end and was far removed from the global or provincial cartography of the time. The frame consists of a narrow moulding which contains a rectangle of hardboard, textured with gesso and colour-washed to taste. This is a chosen size, a kind of mount or matt, larger than the picture. The picture is clipped, with its glass, onto a smaller piece of hardboard and this is glued onto the centre of the frame with its textured backing. The glazed section is raised from its background on two thin strips of wood. The illustrations show the process in cross section. In effect, this frame was made of fairly narrow mouldings with a piece of hardboard cut to fit the rebate.

The picture was trimmed to a rectangle and set on a piece of hardboard of the same size and covered with a piece of glass also of the same size. The trimmed drawing was used to determine the size of the background and the frame that contained it. The larger piece of hardboard was sized and given two coats of gesso. A third coat was combed radially from the centre but the middle area, over which the picture would lie was scraped clean, but not quite as big an area as the picture. Two strips of wood $1 \times \frac{1}{4}$ inch (25×6 mm) and 1 inch (25 mm) shorter than the picture were glued to the background, about an inch (25 mm) in from where the picture would lie. The smaller piece of hardboard was glued in position carefully, on to the two strips and allowed to dry. The picture and glass were then laid on this and fixed with four glass clips, the kind used for unframed but glazed pictures. The purpose of the two $1 \times \frac{1}{4}$ inch (25×6 mm) strips was to raise the picture from the textured background, so that it appeared to 'float', and also to allow space for the glass clips to fit under the smaller piece of hardboard. The degree of isolating texture on the background, the width and nature of the moulding and the general proportions, are matters of judgment and permit many variations, not necessarily similar in general appearance. The example shown has a very light transparent black wash over the background texture, giving a striated grey effect. The effect of some Indian ink greatly thinned with size over a texture is to produce a grey at a distance, but a very lively luminescent grey quite unlike a flat colour. The moulding was in silver, or rather burnished aluminium cast in cold poured resin, and designed and cast to give the effect of a sequence of reflecting highlights, an idea that came from a piece of Bauhaus sculpture. A suitable commercial moulding could have been used.

LUNETTE FRAMES

An object like a painted fan needs to be shown opened, and does not fit easily in a rectangular frame. It is possible, with a little ingenuity, to make a semi-circular or a lunette (less than semicircular) box frame as shown. The degree of ornamentation depends on the fan itself. An 18th-century French fan or an early 19th-century Spanish or Cuban fan can take as much neo-classical or rococo ornament, heavily gilded, as courage allows. East India Company Chinese fans can be either very plain or luxuriously simple in the Chinese manner. The example shown is made from a length of two-by-one (50 × 25 mm), a strip of hardboard 2 inches (50 mm) deep for the bow. This is usually about one-and-a-half times as long as the straight base but make it one-and-three-quarters for safety. Soak the strip in water for three or four hours until it darkens in colour and bend accurately. Pin one end to the butt of the piece of two-by-one (50 × 25 mm) and make a suitable curve, then pin the other end to the end of the two-by-one (50 × 25 mm). The surplus can be sawn off when dry. For safety, wedge a piece of wood from the centre of the straight to the centre of the bow to fit tightly without distortion of the curve. This is removed when the hardboard is dry. Lay the bowed shape on a larger piece of hardboard, mark out its base and cut it out. Pin this to the straight base and fix the bowed part of the base to the bowed strip by cementing a length of 1-inch (25-mm) gauze bandage over the joint, extending $\frac{1}{2}$ inch (12 mm) onto the strip and $\frac{1}{2}$ inch (12 mm) onto the baseboard. It is easier to do this in shorter lengths, 4 to 6 inches (100–150 mm) depending on the curve. Smear contact adhesive on the hardboard, and lay the bandage when still wet. The cement will then penetrate the bandage and bond strongly. In passing, contact adhesives are most easily removed from the finger tips by soaking them in warm water for a minute and then rubbing off the dried cement with a scouring powder. You will now have a bow-shaped box, quite strong, ready for a rebate to fit the glazing.

Glue a strip of $\frac{1}{4} \times \frac{1}{4}$-inch (6 × 6-mm) wood, $\frac{1}{10}$ inch (2·5 mm) down from the top of the straight base, and glue a series of short blocks cut from the same wood to form a discontinuous rebate around the hardboard bow $\frac{1}{10}$ inch (2·5 mm) down from the top. This is the easiest way to get around the curve. Well glued, they will hold firmly. The inside of the box should now be finished off. Glue a second strip of bandage over the inside of the bowed joint to secure it permanently, and tidy up the inside by lining the base and sides up to the rebate in fabric or paper. The fabric on the sides can run up to the top of the rebate, but not on top of it, for the glass must rest there. Since the glazing cannot easily be replaced if broken, it is safer to use one of the available

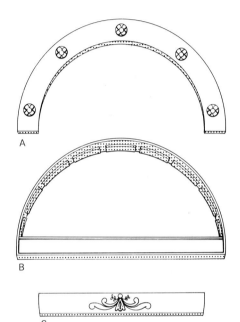

The lunette frame
(A) face of bow
(B) shallow box structure
(C) face of base
(D) assembled parts with gesso, sanding and ornament

transparent plastic sheetings which are cut with a saw and can be trimmed with a file. Care is needed to prevent scratches, always a hazard with plastics, which otherwise have high optical qualities. Any visible part of the rebate strips are better painted black or some dark colour.

At this point fit the fan in place, using looped staples of floral wire, pushed through the baseboard and twisted tightly behind. Lay the glazing in place and give some thought to the finish needed on the face. Using the structure as a measure, draw a curved strip a little over $1\frac{1}{4}$ inches (30 mm) wide and extending across the width of the straight base, that is, extended by 1 inch (25 mm) at either end. A strip of similar width 2 inches (50 mm) shorter than the straight-edge covers the base. Both strips serve to cover the rebate, which is really an upsidedown rebate, and hold the glazing in place, and are cut in hardboard or plywood. Many woodshops will do the cutting for you if you do not have a bandsaw. The plastic glazing should be covered in paper and sticky tape for protection during the finishing.

The hardboard bow facing should be pinned to either end of two-by-one (50 × 25 mm) base and the straight facing pinned down with three or four pins. The joining along the bowed edge should be secured with a strip of 1-inch (25-mm) gauze bandage, as before, with a contact adhesive. This should be done as smoothly and neatly as possible.

When dry, after a thin coat of size and sufficient coats of gesso to cover the joints and the bandage strips, a last coat can be scratched with a plastic nailbrush, possibly in a radial pattern, and vertically on the sides. After gentle sandpapering the gesso can be coloured opaquely or transparently, touched with wax amalgam, gold or silver. A simple form of ornament of a neo-classical kind can be achieved by making a silicone rubber mould of a rosette, roundel, cameo or even a beautiful button, about 1 inch (25 mm) in diameter, stuck at suitable intervals along the face. It is equally possible, but more arduous, to cast from a suitable silicone rubber mould of a moulding. The straight base can be cast in Crystacal but the curved length must be squeezed in gesso pasta and fixed as previously described. It is even possible to cast and fix some sort of corner ornament at either end of the base and a centre ornament in the centre of the bow.

With luck, fractions of larger ornaments can be squeezed from silicone rubber moulds to suit various needs and to give a suitable period effect. A Chinese bowed frame might be either left fairly plain or decorated with roundels as above, abstracted from a Chinese button, piece of jade or whatever is available. When the surfaces have been gessoed white, they can be glazed a pale green with polyester resin, suggesting jade, or Chinese blue, with a lot of white showing.

GEORGIAN PRINT FRAMES

One of the commonest categories in framing consists largely of prints, engravings, woodcuts, maps and the like, from the late 17th century to the middle of the 19th century. Sadly, these are often cut from old books, but the earlier Italian engravings of classical subjects were often issued in loose folios; Piranesi prints or prints of statues from Herculaneum.

Although modern styles of mounting and framing can be devised effectively, the necessarily simple framing benefits from a period touch, as if the print had hung well-preserved for generations on the study wall of an old country house.

Something of this effect can be achieved easily by choosing a deep ivory mount (or matt), even though this might not have been used in the 1780s. The moulding for the frame should be a 1-inch (25-mm) scooped moulding in white wood, easily available, unfinished, in woodshops. Naturally, oak or anything similar will do as well.

Cut and assemble the frame and stain it with a spirit dye to a dark brown if suitable. Sometimes two coats are needed, well rubbed down with steel wool.

Secure from somewhere a small corner ornament and take four squeezes in gesso pasta as described earlier, and fix them, just as before. Small corner ornaments are not easy to find on old frames, but they do exist. Sometimes a section of a larger corner ornament can be used, or a spandrel ornament from the face of a clock or from a piece of silverware. The ornaments should be steel-woolled and trimmed when they are dry and stained so that the colour can be closely matched and the entire frame waxed and polished with lambswool to give a restful antique glow.

If a light colour seems necessary, the wood can be left pale and the pasta tinted by mixing in a little yellow ochre to match the wood. After drying and steel-woolling, the entire frame can be waxed and polished. The effect is still period but, somehow, fresh with a gesture towards modern decor.

Small corner ornaments are extremely useful and can sometimes be found on late 19th-century photograph frames and the like. Frequently, from those eclectic times, the frame, though redolent of Queen Victoria retired to Osborne, or a saucy calf from the Moulin Rouge, contained elements that are purely classical or rococo. These should be garnered and stored whenever possible. The illustration shows an Italian engraving stained dark brown and treated by this simple means.

An 18th-century Italian engraving in a simple scooped frame with small corner ornaments such as were used in old private libraries and studies. The engraving is of Roman actors taken from an antique fresco or mosaic

GLAZING AND COMPLETION

GLAZED FRAMES should be made to fit the mount, never the reverse. Although the completed frame should be a unity of design comprizing picture, mount or matt and frame, in effect the frame has to be made to fit the mount. Glass (18 oz/500 g) is best cut in the glaziers. It is difficult to store in large sheets domestically and is not very economic in limited amounts. For measurement it should be about $\frac{1}{16}$ inch (1·5 mm) smaller than the frame. Over-tight glass can snap in a dry warm room if shrinkage or warping occurs. It is useful to be able to cut a larger faulty piece of glass smaller, to trim it to a smaller frame or picture than was originally intended. For this, a table covered with baize or blanket is needed, and two T-squares, blunt-nosed pliers and a diamond or steel wheel-cutter. The glass must be clean.

T-squares can be made to any convenient length cheaply, and should be slightly longer than the longest cut you can envisage if you are cutting down from spare glass. Effective T-squares can be made from $1\frac{1}{2} \times \frac{1}{4}$-inch (38 × 6-mm) hardwood assembled to a T-shape and glued on one end at an angle of 90°. Plainly this must be accurate. They are used upsidedown, with the cross piece underneath the long bar. Drill a hole for hanging on a nail when not in use. Cement a length of dressmaker's tape-measure along the appropriate edge of each long bar. One T-square is used for length and one for breadth, although these are notional terms. The tape-measures should be checked against a ruler for accuracy since old ones stretch. Cut a little notch in the crossbar on both T-squares to enable the tool to get into the edge of the glass. If a wheel tool is used it should be kept in a jar of methyl alcohol or white spirit (naptha) to prevent rust.

In order to cut the glass, two sides of it should be at right angles. Set the T-square on these and move one against the other until they enclose the chosen size. Allow about $\frac{1}{8}$ inch (3 mm) for the thickness of the base of the glass cutter and check again to ensure that the T-squares are lying 90° true. Take away the horizontal T-square, hold the cutter between the index and middle fingers, balanced by the thumb, inclining slightly towards yourself and cut firmly and quickly from the top to the base of the glass. A cut sounds different from a scratch and must be learnt by practice, listen for a light hiss. A scratch is whiter and is sometimes discontinuous. Bring the cut over the edge of the table and press downwards sharply. Alternatively lay the cut over the long bar of the T-square and press sharply. All cuts are made completely across a given piece of glass. Measure up the other dimension with a T-square and cut again. Cuts near the edge of a sheet sometimes leave serrated fragments which can be removed with a pliers. Rub the rough edges with a carborundum stone.

We have seen how to make mouldings, simple and complex, and

Glass ready for cutting

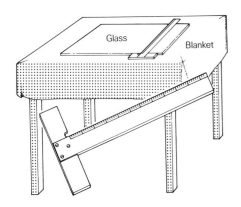

how to cut and assemble them into frame. Ready-made mouldings are cut and assembled similarly. We have also considered mounts (matts) for water-colours, engravings, drawings, lithographs, maps; in other words, artwork on paper which is always covered with glass and sealed from behind for atmospheric protection.

All pictures stretched over a window-mount need a rigid backing cut from mounting board, the same size as the window mount, or the glass for that matter. To finish off all such framing, clean the glass on both sides and lay it in the frame. Place the mounted picture on top of it, face down. The thickness of the window will prevent the picture touching the glass. Lay the backing card on the back of the mounted picture and be satisfied that everything fits. If the glass is slightly too small, but is still capable of covering the frame opening, a few fragments of matchstick, flicked with a contact cement, can be pressed between the edge of the glass and the rebate, where they will hold the glass in position. A few stamp-sized pieces of gummed tape from the back of the card to the back of the frame will do the same thing for a slightly undersized mount. I am talking of no more than $\frac{1}{8}$ inch (3 mm) short measure, which sometimes happens, particularly at first. Before pinning the whole thing into the frame, make sure that no fragments of paper or wood are loose behind the glass.

To drive in the pins use a light hammer and $\frac{5}{8}$-inch (16-mm) or $\frac{3}{4}$-inch (19-mm) moulding or veneer pins every four inches (100 mm) or so. Hold a block of wood ($2 \times 2 \times 8$ inches/$50 \times 50 \times 200$ mm) on the outside of the frame against the rebate, into which you are driving the pin. Lay the pin flat on the card and tap its point into the exposed piece of rebate. Do not drive it in at a descending angle. Drive the pins in about half-way and when they are all home, cover round this edge of the frame with strips of gummed paper, across the pins and onto the card, sealing the picture from anything except damp or excessive heat.

If a total and homogeneous seal is needed for the sake of appearance, a sheet of brown Kraft paper can be pasted over the entire back, frame and backing board with a strong cold water paste. Cut the paper a little larger than needed, paste the frame and backing board and also the paper and tamp the paper down. When dry it can be trimmed off

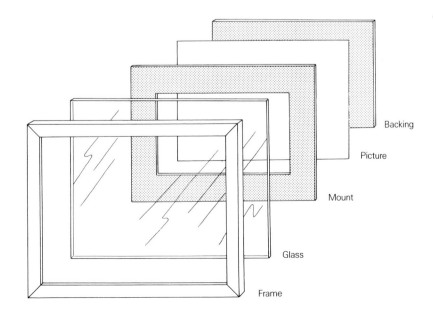

Backing

Picture

Mount

Glass

Frame

The sequence of components in a framed, mounted glazed picture. With oils, omit (usually) glass, mount and backing

A mounted picture before framing

The picture in its frame with backing board and pinning begun

with a knife or by rubbing the edge with a piece of fine sandpaper wrapped around a piece of cardboard 1×3 inches (25×75 mm), the surplus strips of paper will fall away.

Jobbing framers often use a kind of 'gun' which shoots thin flat diamond-shaped brads into the frame on squeezing a trigger, and anyone undertaking a lot of glazed framing might prefer one of these, but framers managed with pins for centuries before such useful tools were available.

Screw eyes, screw rings or D rings are used on the back of the frame to hold the hanging wire. Screw rings and screw eyes vary in size and heavier frames for oil paintings need large ones, about $\frac{1}{2}$ inch (12 mm) in diameter. Start them with a thin awl and screw home, about one-third of the height down from the top. Use light or heavy

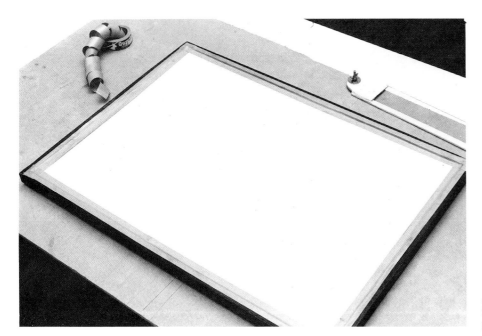

Apply gummed tape from the back of the frame on to the backing board and over the pins

The alcoholic return of Bacchus from India to hang above the port decanter

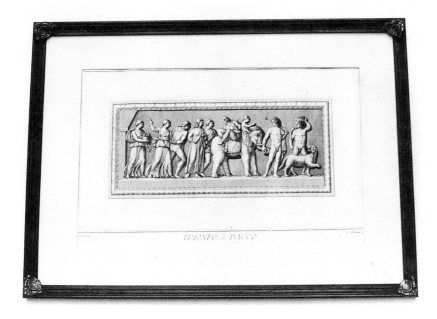

brass-covered picture wire with about 1 inch (25 mm) looseness and always use it double, winding it round itself for a couple of inches to finish off.

D rings are useful when very narrow mouldings are used. These are often too fragile or shallow to take a screw eye. In this case, the backing piece should be cut from the thinnest hardboard and the D rings riveted to it. Nowadays they come in packets complete with rivets. The weight of the picture, glass and frame hang from the hardboard and does not strain the fragile mitres which narrow mouldings necessitate. Indeed, for large pictures with glass, narrow mouldings are dangerous. If self-effacement is needed in the frame, a somewhat wider moulding is safer, and reliance is placed on its texture and colour to keep in the background.

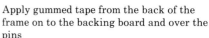

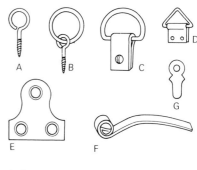

A. Screw eye
B. Screw eye and ring
C. D ring
D. Back hanger

E. Glass plate
F. Steel clip
G. Swing clip

(C) and (D) are rivitted to the backing board.
(E) is for heavy mirrors. (F) is used for small oil canvasses for easy removal of painting.
(G) Used mainly for photographs etc

CONCLUSION

While I have covered the basics of framing in this book to the extent that an assiduous reader should be able to buy the tools and start mounting and framing, I have concentrated on areas of framing and making one's own mouldings not dealt with elsewhere.

Properly followed, it should enable the amateur or the professional to compete with gallery conservationists and bespoke framing experts reasonably well. Indeed, the scope is wider and less tied to conventional market demands. My greatest hopes are pinned on dedicated amateurs who can follow their obsession and devote time and research to the subject. The more of the latter the better.

It should be remembered also that many, though not all ornamented frames can be finished in a manner suitable for modern paintings. I have described thin wash colours over gesso and polyester glazes, but there is much more to be devised and invented. If I were to write this book in a year's time, doubtless the advice could be extended and I hope that some readers will assist in the enterprise, and perhaps I may see some of the results.

Modern moulding designs can be devised. I have used motifs based on Papuan bark cloth, seaweed and even sea surf on which to base rather flat moulding designs, working on flat strips of clay and casting onto wood.

The present movement in painting seems to point in towards the need for richer framing, and since industry seems unlikely to supply it in any aesthetically acceptable form, I hope this book will fill part of this need.

This frame is formed from the outer
moulding of a frame shown on page 43.
Within the picture there are two frames
shown, holding a mirror glass and a small
painting. Both are cast in Crystacal and
wax-gilded. On top is a frame cast from a
19th-century Italian moulding: a form of
rococo adapted to a repeating pattern and
pierced with holes to increase its enrichment
and lightness

LIST OF SUPPLIERS

The following list is largely confined to the more specialised needs mentioned in this book and is particularly convenient to those with some access to the London area. There are, however, regional equivalents in England, Scotland, Wales and Ireland.

Ashworth & Thomson (Nottingham), 77 White Lion Street, London N.1., 01 837 6836, keep a wide stock of plain wood mouldings suitable for finishing. Many woodshops however keep smaller stocks of plain rebated and architectural mouldings.

Brodie & Middleton, Theatrical suppliers, 68 Drury Lane, Covent Garden, London WC2, 01 836 3289 keep a variety of dry pigment colours, analine dyes, gilders whiting, rabbit size and glue size as well as brushes, shellacs and other sundries.

Cornellissen & Sons, Art Colourmen, 22 Great Queen Street, London WC2, 01 405 3304, stock dry pigments and art-related sundries.

Lawrence & Aitken, Cardboard manufacturers, Mountcutters, Albion Works, Kimberley Road, London NW6, 01 624 8135.

John Myland, 57 Farringdon Road, London EC1, 01 352 4705 supply cabinetmakers' requirements, ebonizing liquids, polishes as well as carnauba wax and beeswax.

Ploton, 273 Archway Road, London N6, 01 348 0315 for gilders' supplies.

George Wiley, originally of London, Goldbeaters, now at Firth Road, Houston Industrial Estate, Livingstone, West Lothian, Scotland, 0506 38611 operate a postal service for gilders covering all needs: gold leaf, schlagg and aluminium (silver) leaf, mordants, agates, tips etc.

Finished manufactured mouldings
Magnolia Mouldings, 145 Stoke Newington Church Street, London, N16, 01 249 6961.

D & J Simons, 122 Hackney Road, London E2, 01 729 2751.

W Tanner, 8 Dereham Place, London EC2, 01 739 5597.

BIBLIOGRAPHY

Most books on framing have something useful to say on one aspect or another, but there is practically nothing available on repairing, or reproduction of antique frames or designing mouldings.

The following books from simple to more complex treatments of the subject might prove a useful guide. Non-English books should be available in specialised libraries, eg the Victoria and Albert Museum art library.

Better Frames for your Pictures by Frederick Taubes. Thames & Hudson.

Framing Pictures by J. T. Burns. Charles Scribners & Sons.

Alte Bilderrahmen by Claus Grimm. Callweg Verlag, Munich 1977.

Der Bilderrahmen by Siegfried E. Fuchs. Verlag Aurel Bongers K.G., Recklinghausen.

Prijt de Lijst by P. J. J. Van Thiel. C. J. de Bruyn Kops. Rijksmuseum. 1984.

Handbook of Ornament by Franz Sales Mayer. Dover Books, reprint.

English Looking Glasses: A study of Glass, Frames and Makers by Geoffrey Wills. Country Life Ltd., London.

El Marco en la Historia del Arte and *El Arte de d'Ore*, both by Eugenio Garcia Harranz, Madrid.

GLOSSARY

agate tool
Wooden handle tipped with a semi-precious stone, for burnishing.

antiquing
Giving a softer, worn or venerable appearance.

aquarelle painting
Thin transparent water-colouring.

Armenian bole or Assiette d'oré
Naturally coloured fine clay used as base for gold leaf. Arm. b, in dry lumps, Ass. d'oré ground to paste in water.

Baroque
Prevailing artistic and architectural style in late 17th-century Europe with characteristics of surprise and splendour and having an Olympian certainty.

burnishing
The compression of a finishing surface with a hard tool to give lustre and depth.

burnishing bronze
A bronze powder, simulating gold, which is laid on with size and is capable of being burnished.

burnished water gilding
Gilding in which the leaf is laid on the bole surface with water or size water and polished with an agate tool.

cabochon
A feature in carved ornament, derived from jewellery, resembling a section of a sphere or ovoid.

carnauba wax
An extremely hard brittle wax from a Brazilian palm. A proportion with a softer wax increases the shine after polishing.

carved frame
A frame carved in wood, most commonly Alpine pine or lime.

cast frame
A frame in which the ornament is added to the wood by casting or pressing by hand from a mould.

centre ornament
A heavier proliferation of ornament in the centre of the sides of a frame, characteristic of the Baroque and Rococo styles.

Cavetto (Ital. *Cavare*)
A scooped or spoon curve in the profile of a moulding.

cold poured metal
Fine metal powder amalgamated with polyester resin to produce a durable metal veneer.

corner ornament
A thickening of ornament on the corners of a frame in an orderly manner, characteristic of the Baroque style. Both centre and corner ornaments derived from earlier features in framing and persisted in the later Rococo style.

Crystacal
A hard, white casting plaster used in sculpture, made by British Gypsum. An Alpha-produced, hemi-hydrate gypsum plaster.

curing
The slow development of final characteristics after effective completion.

distressing
The deliberate abrasion of a frame or furniture to suggest use and age. Usually practised to reduce brashness and induce visual reassurance.

double mount or matt
Two mounts or matts laid on top of each other, the uppermost having a slightly larger aperture than the lower.

Dutch metal *see* schlagg leaf.
Empire frame
A rather stark development from the classical Louis XVI frame in France, popular under Napoleon Buonaparte and later elsewhere.

flat
A flat strip or section of a more complex moulding. Also used to describe an inner or inset frame bordering the picture and unattached to the outer frame. It is usually flat sectioned and matt gilded.

fresco
A painting on fresh (fresco) lime plaster using wet pigments.

gesso Italian for gypsum.
A combination of plaster, chalk and glue in a liquid or a putty-like form.

gesso pasta
The putty-like form of above.

gilder's clay
Armenian bole or Assiette d'oré (q.v.).

gilder's tip
A flat, very soft brush, shaped like a comb for lifting gold leaf.

gilder's whiting
Chalk, quarried from a chalk pit, ground and finely sieved.

highlights
The outer extrusions in sculpture or ornament that catch most light.

hot poured metal
Molten metal cast in a mould.

icon
An image, usually Byzantine or Russian.

intaglio moulding
A moulding the main design of which is intaglio, that is engraved or cut into the surface, not raised from it.

Japan gold size
Quick drying mordant or sticky oil for gilding.

mitre
A 45° cut in a piece of wood.

mitre block
A wooden structure with slots to assist the cutting of a mitre.

mitre joint
Two corresponding 45° cuts glued and pinned to form a 90° corner.

oil gilding
The fixing of gold leaf with a sticky oil, slower and more controllable than with Japan gold size, to which it is allied.

ogee
An S-shaped curve common in Gothic architecture and in the cross-section of wooden mouldings, known as Cyma (recta or reversa), depending on whether concave or convex side is uppermost.

ormolu varnish
A varnish for protecting gold leaf.

parchment size
A size or thin glue made by boiling parchment fragments.

pearl glue
Animal glue served in round grains, not sheets, for easier soaking in water.

pull
The result of pressing a malleable substance such as clay or gesso into a mould with a design in reverse to produce a positive, initially non-rigid cast.

rabbit size
Rabbit glue, made from rabbit skins, which looks like brown sugar. Soaked and thinned with water for size.

rebate or rabbit
A groove formed by the overhang on the sight side of a picture or mirror glass frame moulding: covers the edge of picture or glass.

Rococo
Sinuous, sometimes asymmetric style, 1700–1760 in Europe. A humanised sensual development of Baroque.

roundel ornaments
A round flat ornament like a rosette, complete in itself, common in architecture, framing and furniture.

running a moulding
Moving a metal template of a moulding cross-section along a strip of wet plaster or similar substance, adding fresh plaster until the moulding is complete. Commonly used by decorative plasterers on ceiling cornices.

running pattern
A repeated unit of design on a moulding.

Russian tallow
A butter-like substance prepared from hard animal fats.

scumble
A thin layer of paint used to modify a darker paint beneath.

schlagg leaf
Also known as Dutch metal or gilt metal leaf; a variable brass copper zinc alloy in leaf form, used as gold substitute.

sgraffito (Ital)
A design or pattern scratched through a top layer to ground layer beneath.

shooting board
A stepped wooden block which holds a moulding at a 45° angle, enabling a plane to trim the mitre cut.

size
An animal glue thinned to a watery consistency.

spandrel
The triangular areas indicated by an arch or a circle in a rectangular face or wall. An architectural term.

spoon groove moulding
Cavetto; a scooped profile on a moulding.

squeeze
Same as 'pull'. A soft putty-like substance pressed into a reverse mould, and extracted while still malleable as a positive cast.

stucco
A plaster which has been hardened or toughened.

tempera
A pigment bound with egg or, in this context, size; as in 15th-century painting or theatre backdrops.

template or templet
Pattern, stencil or gauge, cut in a thin sheet, used as a guide in shaping objects.

tondo
(Ital. round). A circular painting or relief.

transfer leaf
Gold schlagg or silver leaf fixed to tissue paper for application to a flat sticky surface.

triptych
A painting on three hinged panels.

vernis ormolu
Ormolu varnish.

wax amalgam
Bronze or other metal powders ground into a solution of waxes in mineral or white spirit.

wax burnishing
The susceptibility of the above or to the wax used alone, to burnishing with an agate tool.

wet and dry sandpaper
More properly called waterproof abrasive paper. Commonly used for fine preparation in vehicle respraying after soaking in water. Can be used dry.

yesso pasta
Spanish for gesso pasta (Ital.). A glue, chalk and paper-pulp putty for casting ornaments.

INDEX

I wish to acknowledge courtesies and assistance from George Brandreth, Anne Dunlop and Cresten Doherty in the preparation of this book, and to offer gratitude to Tom Nisbet RHA, who sparked the quest long ago when every goose was a swan and every lass a queen. I am also indebted to many students of all ages whose needs and sympathy fired my energies.

PICTURE CREDITS

All black and white photography by Laurence Bradbury except 24, 92 top, 107.
Francis Lumley Front and back cover, 1, 25, 32/33, 64.
Rose Jones 2/3, 24, 36/37, 40, 49, 52/53, 60/61, 86/87, 90/91, 94/95, 99, 102/103, 107, 113.
Line drawings by Craig Austin and Phil Blakely.
Thanks to Blackman Harvey for supplying frames in 37 bottom and 102 top.